The All-In-One Noom Diet Cookbook

Delicious, Healthy, and Beginner-Friendly

Breakfast, Lunch, and Dinner Recipes for a

Healthier You: Plus, Learn the Easy Stoplight

Color Hack for Faster Results!

Learn Everything You Need to Know About the Noom Diet With This Book! - Find Easy, Healthy, and Yummy Recipes That Will Absolutely Wow Even the Pickiest Eaters

Ever wanted a life-changing diet hack that would transform your physique but was put off by its difficulty?

Are you ready to kick-start your health journey and discover the benefits of a healthier lifestyle?

The Noom diet is a revolutionary diet plan that simplifies the task of creating a lifestyle change. This program is designed to make it easy to **adopt healthier habits and stick with them in the long term!**

This cookbook will make your healthy journey even easier by providing delicious, healthy, and beginner-friendly breakfast, lunch, and dinner recipes that are perfectly portioned and guaranteed to help you eat better and reach your goals.

Experience the power of Noom's stoplight color coding system with this revolutionary cookbook – *identify healthy green meals that are packed with nutritious ingredients, yellow meals which can still be enjoyed in moderation, and red meals which should be avoided when possible.*

Discover:

- **The easiest diet plan ever!:** With the stoplight color hack, you'll be able to easily identify which foods to eat more of, and which to stay away from.

- **Recipes that aren't hard on the wallet:** You don't have to hunt for special, rare, or expensive food items with these recipes. You have everything you need in your pantry!

- **A healthier, happier you:** Finally achieve all your fitness goals and feel rest assured that you're living your best possible life.

- And more!

Stay healthy while satisfying your taste buds with this unique collection of breakfast, lunch, and dinner recipes fit for any skill level. Each meal is budget-friendly and easy to prepare but still jam-packed with flavor!

So, what are you waiting for?

Scroll up, Click on "Buy Now", and Get Your Copy Now!

Contents

BONUS:
THANK YOU

As a thank you for purchasing one of my books...
I, Samantha Clark, offer you a
FREE BONUS!!

DISCOVER

Fast & Flavorful Recipes for Busy Cooks:

Quick and Easy Meal Solutions for Your Busy

Lifestyle

What are you waiting for? Scan the QR code now!

Or Visit: samanthaclarkbooks.com

Introduction

How often have you tried to lose weight, failing miserably and beating yourself up for it? Perhaps you succeeded after doing some fad diet or performing some other bizarre activity only to regain weight again? Most people have similar experiences with losing weight and eating healthy - it is either too costly or unsustainable. While many methods can be used to lose weight, few are sustainable and can show good results. The Noom diet is a method of losing weight that is sustainable and easy on the pocket.

Different apps and diets often try to help you stay on track by making you track everything all the time. While this is a great approach, many people fail because this does not change their habits. Compared to this method, the Noom program can change your life as it affects your habits and helps you change them through psychology. This is why Noom is currently one of the top-rated apps for losing weight and maintaining weight.

While the Noom app is self-sufficient, this book can help you take things further. It contains an in-depth overview of the app and the program, making it quite comprehensive and interesting. With the combination of recipes and data, the book can help you get started and stay on your weight loss journey until the results are achieved.

The book features basic briefs about the app and the program. It features extensive data on the color-coded program and charts out the various foods you can have on the diet and then categorizes them according to the colors. It also features an extensive chapter on the pros and cons of the diet so that you can make an informed choice about the diet and whether it is suitable for you. Along with this, the book also contains various recipes divided into many categories. These recipes are not only healthy, but they are also delicious. They can be customized according to your tastes and requirements.

So why wait? Read on to learn more about the app that can change your life!

Chapter 1:

Hands-On to the Noom Mindset

Are you struggling with how to lose weight? Have you tried everything but can't find a solution to your problem? Then don't worry; technology is here with answers. Technology in the form of the Noam app can help you stay on track, track your diet, exercise regularly, and motivate you from time to time. Noom is a top-rated and highly celebrated app that can help you lose weight.

According to the Noom website, it is the 'last weight loss program you will ever need.' It is a combination of a health coach, a trainer, and a nutritionist all in one app, and is a fitness and weight loss program that allows you to gain sustainable results that last a lifetime. It uses psychological principles to guide and direct your mind so that you can lose weight, be fit, and eat healthily. In fact, according to TechCrunch, as of May 2021, this app has been downloaded more than 45 million times across 100 nations. These nations include Canada, the United States of America, the United Kingdom, Ireland, Australia, and New Zealand.

Unlike other diet and fitness programs, Noom is driven by psychology, which is why it produces long-lasting and proper results. Unlike other diets, there are no restrictions on food or eating windows that you have to follow in this diet. It is a highly personalized diet for weight loss plan available as an app on your phone. It can help you reach your personal weight goals with ease. This regime focuses on regular exercise, healthy eating, better sleep hygiene, and stress management.

One of the main aspects of the Noom weight loss program is diet. You need to have a proper diet so that you can lose weight in a healthy way. In Noom, diet is not just related to tracking calories and meal plans; it is also concerned with other aspects of health and diet. The Noom app is an integral part of the overall program as it allows you to get support from health coaches and helps you track your fitness. The Noom app tries to incorporate behavioral changes relevant to weight loss and diet. It shows you various food items that are suitable for you to eat. Instead of taking the fear approach, this app tries to instill confidence, educate you about foods and helps you learn how to make more informed and balanced choices. It also promotes healthy reading habits by suggesting facts and tidbits about healthy lifestyles.

Once you begin to change your behaviors, the app also rewards you. You also have constant positive reinforcement as the app has social support. It has been found that accountability and reinforcement are great ways to stick to a plan and follow it for sustained and long-term success. It removes the need for anxiety associated with dieting and focuses on an educational approach instead. The app asks patrons to read articles about good habits and allows you to score your motivation before testing you.

The testing may sound quite daunting, but the app can help you lose weight with lasting results. It depends on the user regarding how much time they want to spend on the app. Some people dedicate only five minutes, while more people can spend around sixteen minutes on the app.

Once you spend two days on the app, you'll be assigned a coach who will check on you every two weeks. The coach will also motivate you and help you understand your health's importance. You will also be added to a group chat and will have a group coach as well. The talk in the chat will be moderated while the group coach will provide continuous remarks, postings, inquiries, and advice. The National Consortium has approved the coaches hired by Noom for credentialing, which makes them quite good.

The users are provided with a daily calorie goal that they must meet. You need to input all the meals or food/drink items consumed throughout the day in the app. You also need to log your physical activity in the app. The Noom app also has a step meter, which allows you to record the number of steps you walk in a day. The app also recommends regularly tracking your water intake, blood pressure, and other health indicators.

A typical Noom membership is supposed to be four months; however, users have reported much better and sustained results with a twelve-month subscription.

Colors and the Noom Diet

The Noom Diet categorizes foods into three categories according to the color green, yellow, and red. Green foods are considered the best, whereas the foods that contain the least amount of nutrients are red. It is recommended to have as many green foods as possible and reduce the number of red foods.

Green Foods

All the food items with low calories that can still satiate you are considered a part of the green color category. The green category includes various fruits and vegetables, egg whites, white fish, non-fat Greek yogurt, rolled oats, quinoa, tofu, salsa, shrimp, unsweetened milk substitutes, and various other healthy food items.

Green foods are considered to be good for your health, and you can make a wide variety of dishes using them, including salads, tacos, green bowls, and other similar recipes.

Green foods also include whole grains such as brown rice and vegetables such as sweet potatoes and carrots.

Yellow Foods

Yellow foods are slightly lower quality than green foods and thus should be consumed moderately. These food items include lean proteins such as salmon, grilled chicken, and turkey breast and low-fat dairy products such as cheese, milk, etc. It also includes healthy fats such as olives and avocados, eggs, grains, beans, legumes, quinoa, chickpeas, etc.

Red Foods

They are also known as red-label foods. While nothing is off-limits in the Noom diet, consuming very low amounts of food under the red category is recommended. The quantity and frequency of these food items should be low. This category includes food items such as processed foods, processed meats, oils, nut butter, condiments, pizza, sugar, French fries, fast food, etc.

Importance of the Noom Plan

The Noom plan is proven to work; however, to get the most out of the program, you must regularly log in your food and water consumption and physical exertion. This way, your coach can keep an eye on you, and you will surely lose weight. It is also necessary to be consistent regarding meal planning and talk to your coach from time to time.

There are many different benefits of the Noom program. Some of these benefits include:

Certified Health Coaches

Noom app features health coaches who must undergo extensive four-week training from the company before joining the program. This training focuses on CBT or cognitive behavioral therapy along with weight-management techniques. The Noom program is based on the psychological principle of cognitive behavioral therapy, which will be explained briefly in the next point.

Psychological Method

Unlike other weight loss methods, the Noom method is based on cognitive behavioral therapy. This therapy focuses on your feelings about your fitness, food, and wellness. It also helps you identify how to turn these feelings and thoughts into actionable methods. This method can allow you to understand the connection between your behaviors, thoughts, and feelings.

Long-Term and Sustainable Results

As the Noom method is based on a psychological approach, the results gained from this diet are much more long-lasting and sustainable. The app focuses on changing habits and does not promote rapid weight loss methods. Instead, it focuses on slow yet steady weight loss, which can be long-lasting and sustainable. It can surely affect your mindset and allow you to focus on overall wellness, fitness, and food.

Whole Foods

The Noom program focuses on eating fresh and whole foods, which means you do not have to buy pre-made shakes, frozen meals, protein bars, or other similar products. Whatever you eat in this diet will satisfy your taste buds, body, and diet. The color method of the diet allows you to choose good food easily and without sacrificing the taste.

All-in-One

What makes Noom better than many other apps and weight loss programs is that it combines a nutritionist, health coach, accountability buddy, and personal trainer all at once. Noom can help you delete many unnecessary apps thanks to its singular focus and all-in-one support system.

Scientific Backing

Various scientific studies prove that the Noom method does work. Some studies that prove the effectiveness of the Noom plan include the following:

According to a study of more than 35,000 people, it was found that around 77% of the people using the Noom app had lost weight within nine months of usage (Chin S et al., 2016)

In another 2016 study done by the National Diabetes Prevention Program, it was found that users reported experiencing weight loss within 16-24 months of usage (Michaelides, A et al., 2016)

Another study done in 2017 found that users lost around 7.5% of their body fat within 12 weeks of using the app. This fat loss was maintained and sustained. This study also proved that the psychological backing of the app truly works and can lead to significant weight loss if followed properly (Toro-Ramos, T et al., 2017)

How to Use this Book

This book covers a detailed analysis of the Noom diet, the basics of the diet, the types of foods you can eat on this diet, the app, how to use the app, and how to follow the diet properly. It also focuses on how to use the support community of the Noom diet and shows how you can use the Noom diet for weight loss and management. It also gives a detailed analysis of the pros and cons of the Noom diet, which will help you make an informed choice about whether you should do the Noom diet. Along with the informative part, this book contains extensive chapters containing mouth-watering recipes. For the ease of the readers, the recipes have been divided into multiple categories so that you can choose whatever you want to make with ease.

This book is suitable for anyone who wants to lose weight and learn about the Noom lifestyle. It is recommended to consult a doctor before you begin any new diet or lifestyle regime, as it may be quite harmful if done improperly.

Common Issues and Mistakes to Consider before You Start Noom

Here are a few common mistakes you must avoid while adopting the Noom diet.

Dishonesty

If you are dishonest to yourself and your coach while doing this regimen, you will not lose any weight and will only lose a lot of money and time. Try to be as honest as possible while logging your data in Noom. Try to be critical and address gaps or faults, if any.

Inconsistency

Consistency and dedication are the keys to losing weight. You will not lose weight if you are inconsistent with your diet and exercise. Change takes time; allow yourself to be consistent and dedicated so that you will start seeing a difference with time.

Not Eating Enough

The Noom diet is not about restricting yourself; you need to consume enough calories, so your metabolism works properly, and you will continue to lose weight. If you don't eat enough calories, your body may go into starvation mode, leading to weight gain. Noom provides a proper calorie budget according to your requirements, making it easy to lose weight. This is why tracking the food and consuming enough calories is necessary.

Myths

There are myths about Noom on social media and the Internet trying to prove how Noom is the Devil incarnate. These articles, posts, etc., are just myths and anecdotes, and most have no scientific backing. The benefits of Noom have been scientifically proven, proving that it works and can provide many health benefits along with weight loss.

Chapter 2:

Learning about the Noom Diet

The best diet is not a diet at all! The Noom app is a psychology-backed diet and health regime that can help you lose weight and become healthy. It allows you to change your behavior and helps you lose weight through psychology. Here are a few facts that you need to know about the Noom diet and app.

What Is Noom?

Noom is quite different from a traditional diet as it is a subscription-based service that helps you make healthy and significant changes in your day-to-day life. These changes can help you live a healthier and more active life.

Many people believe Noom to be a recent fad or app; however, it has been on the market for a long time. It first appeared on the app stores in 2008, albeit back then, it was just a simple calorie and fitness tracker. With time new things were incorporated into the app, and in 2016 it became a subscription-based service that uses the principles of cognitive behavioral therapy. It also incorporates personal coaches, support, and chat groups for added benefits. It features a team of health experts well-versed in diabetes, weight loss, oncology, weight management, hypertension, and psychology. It enables people to take up a lifestyle that can produce sustainable and long-lasting results.

Noom helps users focus on their mindset, which helps them lose and manage weight efficiently. It asks users to be dedicated, focused, and determined. It changes the neural connection in your brain over time and thus changes your habits completely. It works by asking you to examine your eating behaviors. Your emotions related to eating, food, and exercise make you feel accountable and allow you to make significant life changes that can lead to sustainable weight loss.

How Does Noom Work?

The first thing that you need to do when starting the Noom diet plan is to answer a questionnaire. This detailed questionnaire helps the app understand your mental and physical condition, which is used to devise a perfectly curated and personalized plan for you.

Customized Plan

You need to take a 10-minute online quiz once you start the Noom diet. This quiz includes questions about your gender, height, weight, age, and other aspects, such as why you want to lose weight. It also incorporates questions regarding your eating habits and patterns, your activity, and whether you are susceptible to certain health issues such as heart disease, diabetes, depression, etc.

It also has more detailed questions such as 'Has anything led to significant weight gain in recent years?' or 'Why do you feel uncertain about losing weight?' etc. These questions help the app understand your behaviors and habits, which helps personalize a plan.

Downloading the App

Once the quiz is done and you have decided to join the program, you must pay the subscription fee and then download the app. Currently, the app is available on IOS and Android. It can be installed on smartphones and tablets; however, it works much better on a smartphone than on a tablet. Once you have installed the app, you will be asked to sign up using the email address that you used to sign up to join the program.

Commitment Matters

Once you have joined the program, the app will ask you to complete mini-lessons in psychology for 16 weeks. You can choose to spend between five and 16 minutes daily on the plan; five minutes is the absolute minimum. After two days of spending time on the app, you will be connected with a goal coach who will help you by reaching out to you twice a week just so that he can check on you and send you motivational messages. The goal coach will also enquire about your progress from time to time.

After a few days, you will be assigned a peer group and a group coach. The group coach is responsible for moderating the peer group chat. The coach also posts weight loss tips from time to time and may also respond to individual posts.

The calorie restriction of each individual or user is based on the information they provide the app. The restrictions and plans change according to the person. For instance, for pre-diabetic and obese people, Noom has a diabetes prevention program. This program is the first mobile health program recognized by the Centers for Disease Control or CDC, and it can show results for people with Type 2 diabetes.

A personalized plan contains a daily calorie budget. It also asks you to record your physical activity and your meals daily from time to time.

You must also read a few short articles on mindful eating, positive eating, stress relief, and other similar ideas daily.

Noom also has a step counter so you can keep an eye on how many steps you take throughout the day- if you carry your phone with you all the time. The app also asks you to log in your water intake, blood pressure readings, and blood glucose levels from time to time.

The Noom plan is generally designed to last for 16 weeks; however, it is recommended to do an annual plan instead for more sustained results.

What Foods Can You Eat on the Noom Diet?

Nothing is ruled out or banned in the Noom diet. That's right; you can eat whatever you want without worrying about the diet. It is your choice if you want to put any restrictions on food. The app also has options for people who follow a gluten-free, vegan, or low-carb diet. No food is off-limits in the Noom diet.

The Noom principle is that the calories in the food do not direct how satiated or full you feel; the weight of the food makes you full. This is why the Noom folks have devised a color-coded system that categorizes foods according to caloric density or CD. The equation is simple. If the food has high amounts of water, it will have a low caloric density. Foods with low caloric density will make you feel satiated faster without pumping your body unnecessary calories.

Here are the categories according to the colors:

- **Green Foods:** These include all low-calorie yet nutrient-dense food items such as vegetables, fruits, whole grains, etc. These food items are higher in water content and should be consumed in abundance.

- **Yellow Foods:** These food items contain more calories and fewer nutrients than the green category foods, and can be eaten in moderation. They include legumes, lean meats, low-fat dairy items, etc.

- **Red Foods:** These include food items that are highly calorie-dense and have the least amount of necessary nutrients. These items include processed foods, red meats, full-fat cheese, etc. While you can consume these food items, it is recommended to keep them in moderation.

Nothing is restricted or off-limits in the Noom diet plan. It never asks you to stop eating 'red' foods altogether; however, it does ask you to be more mindful while consuming them and avoiding overeating them. Whenever you log food in Noom, it is automatically classified in one of the three categories, which allows you, the user, to understand what needs to be improved and worked upon.

How Much Does Noom Cost?

Noom is available as a free one-week trial; however, it is a subscription-based service. The plan is highly individualized and changes according to the users' requirements. There are many discount codes available that can reduce the price of the plans quite significantly. You can also sign up for annual plans, which will lower the prices.

Types of Foods

While the types of foods in Noom have been covered briefly earlier, here is a more detailed look at the diet.

The Noom diet, as said earlier, is a weight loss program based on psychology. It follows the tenets of psychology and believes that true weight loss is only possible with balance. The diet is available in three categories – green, yellow, and red. As said earlier, green foods are the best for you; yellow foods are okay, while red foods contain the greatest number of calories. It is recommended to have high amounts of green foods, moderate amounts of yellow foods, and low amounts of red foods in your diet.

These categories are not strict guidelines or rules. They are a framework that can help you devise your meal plans easily. Red foods are not excluded from the diet; instead, the color guide can be used as a portion guide. This means desserts (red food) are okay; you just need to consume them moderately.

What Are Green Foods?

Green foods include almost all vegetables and fruits. These food items have a low-calorie density and high water content. This makes them good for feeling full quickly, and that too on very few calories. The food items present on this list are rich in nutrients. Along with fruits and vegetables, this category also contains quinoa, whole-grain items, salsa, rolled oats, unsweetened milk alternatives, tofu, egg whites, white fish, and non-fat Greek yogurt, among many other similar options.

You can think of the Noom diet as a traffic light. Greenlight is considered good to go. Similarly, the food items that fall in the green category of the Noom diet are fine to be eaten in large quantities. Noom encourages people to eat as many green food items as possible while staying within their daily calorie limits.

What Are Yellow Foods?

According to Noom, a rounded meal often is a combination of green foods and yellow foods. Most yellow foods have high amounts of proteins. Yellow foods have more calories and fewer nutrients than green foods, but you can still consume them in moderation. These food items include starches, lean meats, grilled chicken, turkey breast, salmon, tuna, lean beef, etc. For vegetarians and non-meat eaters, the yellow food group contains chickpeas, black beans, eggs, etc. You can also eat avocado, Greek yogurt, whole-grain tortillas, low-sodium canned soups, popcorn, instant potatoes, etc.

What Are Red Foods?

These food items are the most calorie-dense and have low nutrients. While it is okay to eat them, it is recommended to keep them as low as possible. This group of food items includes oils such as avocado, olive, and coconut oil, seeds such as flaxseeds, chia seeds, sunflower seeds, etc., nuts and nut butter such as peanut butter, walnuts, almonds, coconut butter, cashews, etc., desserts such as cookies, pies, cakes, etc., and red meats. The red category also includes food items such as dried fruits, jerky, frozen entrees, crackers, protein powders, bagels, etc.

While you may consume these food items, it is recommended to keep them in moderation but not to feel guilty if you eat them on occasion.

Drinks and the Noom Diet

Water is the most important drink for any diet. The Noom diet, too, is focused on water, which is why it highly promotes green foods over other foods. Other drinks, such as beer, coffee, tea, wine, soda, etc., are generally found in the red and yellow groups. While fruit juice is supposed to be quite healthy and tasty, it contains high amounts of sugar, which is why it is a red food item. Black coffee and tea are okay, as they contain almost zero calories, provided you don't load them up with sugar and cream.

Evidence

Numerous personal and professional pieces of evidence prove that the Noom app works.

In a 2016 study, it was found that the Noom app could be used as a tool for weight loss as well as weight management. Around 35,921 users were tested, of which almost 78% reported weight loss.

Another study found that the Noom app can reduce the risk of diabetes for obese and prediabetes users.

Personal Stories

Social media and the Internet are full of personal stories of people using the Noom app and how the regime has changed their lives. These stories are also available as reviews on the app store and can inspire you to focus more on your diet. (Toro-Ramos, T, et al 2017)

How to Get Started

What Can I Eat?

Like many other programs for weight loss, the Noom diet asks you to track your meals daily. But unlike other programs, this diet does not ask you to cut off anything from your diet. The color-coded system of eating should serve as a general guide for people following the Noom diet. It is recommended that the users consume at least 45% of their daily calorie budget from the yellow group, 30% from the green group, and 25% from the red or orange group. Remember, the red group is not all bad, and the green is not the only good color. Eating too much of any group is bound to produce negative results regardless. Here is a detailed list according to colors:

Green Foods

- **Vegetables:** Mushrooms, lettuce, carrots, spinach, broccoli, asparagus, potatoes, onions, sweet potatoes, cucumbers, bell peppers, peas, Brussels sprouts

- **Fruits:** Kiwi, tomatoes, strawberries, watermelon, grapes, oranges, blueberries, apples, bananas, raspberries, pears, pineapple, peaches, cherries, mango, figs

- **Dairy:** Non-fat milk and cheese, Greek yogurt, sour cream, eggs, cottage cheese

- **Whole grains:** Whole grain pasta, whole grain rice, whole wheat bread, rolled oats, quinoa, brown rice, barley, grits

- **Lean proteins:** Prawns, shrimp, mahi mahi, oysters, tofu

- **Beverages**: Almond milk, skim milk, soy milk, cashew milk, vegetable juice, tomato juice, soy milk

- **Condiments:** Vinegar, salsa, tomato juice, tomato sauce, sauerkraut, citrus juice

These products can be consumed in bigger portions and incorporated in large amounts in your daily meals.

Yellow Foods

These food items can be consumed in moderation. They include

- **Lean Protein:** Fish, turkey, steak, pork, chicken breast, lamb, sushi, canned tuna.

- **Fruits:** Dried apricots, olives, canned pineapples, prunes, plantain, avocado

- **Dairy:** Low-fat yogurt, low-fat cheese, 2% low-fat milk, low-fat cottage cheese

- **Snacks**: Fruit cup, rice pudding, banana pancake, Hummus, acai bowl

- **Beverages:** Ginger beer, vodka soda, diet soda, light beer, grapefruit juice, orange juice, unsweetened cranberry juice, fruit smoothie

- **Legumes:** Edamame, lentils, baked and refried beans, chickpeas, tempeh

- **Condiments:** Oyster sauce, cacao powder, gravy, balsamic vinegar, soy sauce, mustard, pizza sauce

Red Foods

- **Fruits:** Dates, raisins, dried cranberries

- **Grains:** Biscuits, white bread, pita bread, flour tortillas, hot dog buns, croissants, granola, bagels, waffles, muffins

- **Dairy:** Margarine, butter, whole milk, full-fat cheese, cream cheese, half and half, full-fat yogurt, cottage cheese

- **Condiments:** Ranch dressing, mayonnaise, sour cream, olive oil, barbecue sauce, ketchup, pesto, maple syrup, honey, coconut milk

- **Snacks:** Tortilla chips, nuts, crackers, potato chips, popcorn, pretzels

- **Desserts:** Dark chocolate, sugar, cookies, ice cream, apple pie, cake, cheesecake, candy, whipped cream

- **Beverages:** White wine, red wine, champagne, vodka, coffee creamers, margarita, mixed coffee, apple cider

The red food group contains food items high in saturated fats, calories, sugar, sodium, and processed carbs. You can have these foods, but avoiding them as much as possible is recommended.

Chapter 3:

"Good Will"

Helping others without expectation of anything in return has been proven to lead to increased happiness and satisfaction in life.

I would love to give you the chance to experience that same feeling during your reading or listening experience today...

All it takes is a few moments of your time to answer one simple question:

Would you make a difference in the life of someone you've never met—without spending any money or seeking recognition for your good will?

If so, I have a small request for you.

If you've found value in your reading or listening experience today, I humbly ask that you take a brief moment right now to leave an honest review of this book. It won't cost you anything but 30 seconds of your time—just a few seconds to share your thoughts with others.

Your voice can go a long way in helping someone else find the same inspiration and knowledge that you have.

Are you familiar with leaving a review for an Audible, Kindle, or e-reader book? If so, it's simple:

If you're on **Audible**: just hit the three dots in the top right of your device, click rate & review, then leave a few sentences about the book along with your star rating.

If you're reading on **Kindle** or an e-reader, simply scroll to the last page of the book and swipe up—the review should prompt from there.

If you're on a **Paperback** or any other physical format of this book, you can find the book page on Amazon (or wherever you bought this) and leave your review right there.

Chapter 4:

Breakfast Recipes

Overnight Oats

Serves: 1

Nutritional values per serving: For base recipe (without optional flavorings)

Calories: 194

Fat: 5 g

Carbohydrate: 30 g

Protein: 7 g

Ingredients:

For the base recipe:

- ¼ cup old-fashioned rolled oats

- ⅛ cup plain non-fat yogurt

- ½ tablespoon honey or maple syrup

- ⅛ teaspoon pure vanilla extract

- ¼ cup non-fat milk or soy milk or any milk of your choice

- A dash of salt

- ½ tablespoon chia seeds

For nutty berry flavor: Optional

- ¼ cup fresh berries of your choice, chopped

- ⅛ cup chopped nuts of your choice

For chocolate flavor: Optional

- 1 teaspoon cocoa powder or more to taste

- ⅛ cup chopped nuts (optional)

For peanut butter flavor: Optional

- ½ tablespoon smooth, natural peanut butter or more to taste

For banana bread flavor: Optional

- 1 banana, chopped

- ⅛ cup chopped walnuts (optional)

- ⅛ teaspoon ground cinnamon

Directions:

1. To make base oatmeal: Combine milk, vanilla, chia seeds, salt, oats, yogurt, and honey in a bowl.

2. Keep the bowl covered in the refrigerator for 4 – 8 hours.

3. Stir and serve.

4. To make flavored oatmeal: Add the chosen flavoring options in step 3 and serve.

Berry Quinoa Breakfast Bowls

Serves: 1

Calories: 376

Fat: 8 g

Carbohydrate: 55 g

Protein: 24 g

Ingredients:

- ¼ cup uncooked quinoa, rinsed

- A dash of salt

- ⅛ teaspoon vanilla extract or almond extract

- ¼ cup plain non-fat Greek yogurt

- 1 tablespoon slivered almonds, toasted

- ½ cup low-fat milk

- 2 teaspoons maple syrup, divided

- ⅛ teaspoon ground cinnamon

- ½ cup chopped strawberries

Directions:

1. Pour the milk into a saucepan and place it over medium-low heat.

2. When the milk is hot, stir in salt and quinoa. When the mixture starts boiling, turn the heat to low and cook covered for about 5 – 8 minutes.

3. Add 1 teaspoon of maple syrup and cinnamon and stir. Continue cooking covered until dry, stirring often, and then transfer it to a bowl.

4. Combine yogurt, vanilla, and 1 teaspoon of maple syrup in a bowl. Pour the mixture over the quinoa.

5. Scatter almonds and strawberries on top and serve.

Chia Pudding

Serves: 2

Nutritional values per serving: 1 bowl, without toppings

Calories: 159

Fat: 9 g

Carbohydrate: 16 g

Protein: 5 g

Ingredients:

- 1 cup non-fat or non-dairy milk of your choice

- ½ teaspoon maple syrup

- 1 tablespoon chia seeds

- ¼ teaspoon vanilla extract

- Topping of your choice

Directions:

1. The night before: Combine milk, chia seeds, maple syrup, and vanilla in a bowl. Cover and let it rest for 15 minutes.

2. Give the mixture a good stir and place it covered in the refrigerator all night.

3. The following morning, stir the pudding well and divide it into two bowls. Serve with toppings of your choice.

Sweet Potato Protein Breakfast Bowl

Serves: 2

Nutritional values per serving: 1 bowl, without optional toppings

Calories: 273

Fat: 3 g

Carbohydrate: 43 g

Protein: 23 g

Ingredients:

- 2 small sweet potatoes

- 2 small bananas, sliced

- ½ cup blueberries

- ½ cup raspberries

- 2 scoops egg white protein powder

Toppings: Optional

- Hemp hearts

- Chia seeds

- Any other toppings of your choice

Directions:

1. Preheat the oven to 425° F. Line a baking sheet with a sheet of aluminum foil.

2. Pierce a few holes in the sweet potatoes and place them on the foil.

3. Place the baking sheet in the oven and bake for 40 – 50 minutes or until fork tender.

4. When the sweet potatoes cool slightly, peel them and place them in a bowl. Mash using a fork.

5. Add protein powder and stir.

6. Divide the sweet potato mash into two bowls, and place the fruits on top. Add optional toppings if using and serve warm or cold.

Pumpkin Smoothie

Serves: 1

Calories: 170

Fat: 0 g

Carbohydrate: 40 g

Protein: 4 g

Ingredients:

- ¼ cup pumpkin puree

- 6 tablespoons fat-free vanilla yogurt or Greek vanilla yogurt

- ¼ teaspoon pumpkin pie spice

- ½ cup crushed ice

- ¼ medium very ripe banana, sliced

- ½ tablespoon honey

- ⅛ teaspoon pure vanilla extract

Directions:

1. Put the pumpkin puree, yogurt, pumpkin pie spice, ice, banana, honey, and vanilla in a blender and process until smooth.

2. Pour into a glass and serve.

Berry Lime Smoothie

Serves: 1

Calories: 150

Fat: 1 g

Carbohydrate: 36 g

Protein: 2.6 g

Ingredients:

- 1 cup of berries of your choice
- ¼ cup orange juice, unsweetened
- ¼ cup crushed ice
- ½ ripe banana, sliced
- ½ tablespoon lime juice
- Mint sprig to garnish

Directions:

1. Blend berries, orange juice, ice, banana, and lime juice in a blender until smooth.

2. Pour into a glass and serve garnished with mint sprig.

Raspberry Smoothie

Serves: 1

Calories: 224

Fat: 1 g

Carbohydrate: 34 g

Protein: 8 g

Ingredients:

- ¾ cup apple juice
- ¾ cup frozen raspberries
- ½ tablespoon honey
- ½ ripe banana, sliced
- 6 tablespoons non-fat vanilla Greek yogurt
- Fresh raspberries to garnish
- Mint sprig to garnish

Directions:

1. Blend the apple juice, raspberries, honey, banana, and yogurt until smooth.

2. Pour into a glass and serve garnished with raspberries and mint sprig.

Berry-Licious Smoothie Bowl

Serves: 2

Nutritional values per serving: 1 bowl

Calories: 317

Fat: 12 g

Carbohydrate: 54 g

Protein: 7 g

Ingredients:

- 1 cup raspberries
- 12 strawberries, chopped
- 1 cup blueberries
- 2 medium bananas, sliced
- 1 cup almond milk
- 2 tablespoons almond butter
- Berries to garnish
- Banana slices to garnish

Directions:

1. Blend the berries, banana, milk, and almond butter until thick and smooth.

2. Divide into two bowls. Place berries and banana slices on top and serve.

Acai Bowl

Serves: 1

Nutritional values per serving: 1 bowl without toppings

Calories: 248

Fat: 10 g

Carbohydrate: 29 g

Protein: 7 g

Ingredients:

- ½ banana, sliced, frozen
- ¼ cup frozen strawberries
- ¼ cup frozen blueberries
- 6 tablespoons milk of your choice or apple juice
- 1 packet (3.5 ounces) frozen acai puree, break into pieces
- ¼ cup plain non-fat yogurt
- Toppings of your choice

Directions:

1. Blend the fruits, milk, acai puree, and yogurt until smooth.
2. Pour into a bowl and serve.

Avocado Toast

Serves: 2

Nutritional values per serving: 1 avocado toast, without toppings

Calories: 237

Fat: 15.8 g

Carbohydrate: 21.4 g

Protein: 6.1 g

Ingredients:

- 2 thick slices of whole-grain bread

- Salt to taste

- 1 ripe avocado, peeled, pitted, mashed

- Toppings of your choice (optional)

Directions:

1. Toast the bread slices until crisp and brown.

2. Mash the avocado to the desired texture, add salt and stir.

3. Spread half the avocado on each toast. Add toppings if using and serve.

Maple Turkey Sausage

Serves: 3

Nutritional values per serving: 1 patty

Calories: 95

Fat: 1 g

Carbohydrate: 3 g

Protein: 18 g

Ingredients:

- ½ pound ground turkey
- ½ teaspoon sea salt
- ⅛ teaspoon crushed red pepper flakes
- ¼ teaspoon dried thyme
- ½ tablespoon maple syrup
- ⅛ teaspoon black pepper
- ¼ teaspoon garlic powder
- ¼ teaspoon dried sage

Directions:

1. Combine turkey, seasonings, thyme, and maple syrup in a bowl.

2. Divide the mixture into three equal pieces and shape them into patties. You can moisten your hands with water while shaping the patty to prevent sticking.

3. Place a nonstick pan over medium heat. Spray the pan lightly with some cooking oil spray.

4. When the pan is hot, place the patties in the pan and cook until the underside is brown for about 7 to 8 minutes. Flip the patties over. Flatten the patties by pressing them with a spatula and cook the other side for 7 to 8 minutes or until the internal temperature of the patty shows 165° F on the meat thermometer.

5. If at any time you think the patties are getting brown very quickly, reduce the heat.

6. Serve.

7. You can store them in the refrigerator for about 4 days in an airtight container.

Breakfast Sandwiches

Serves: 3

Nutritional values per serving: 1 sandwich

Calories: 226

Fat: 8 g

Carbohydrate: 25 g

Protein: 15 g

Ingredients:

- ¾ cup egg whites, beaten lightly

- 3 multigrain or whole-wheat English muffins, split

- Everything bagel seasoning to taste

- 3 frozen chicken or turkey sausage patties

- 3 slices low-fat cheese of your choice

Directions:

1. Preheat the oven to 350° F.

2. Take a donut pan and grease 3 holes with cooking oil spray.

3. Scatter seasoning into each hole, and add ¼ cup of egg whites to each one.

4. Place the donut pan in the oven and cook for 15 minutes or until the whites are set.

5. Heat the sausage patty following the directions given on the

package.

6. Toast the muffin halves if desired.

7. Place a patty, baked egg, and a cheese slice between each English muffin and serve.

Egg White Muffins

Serves: 6

Nutritional values per serving: 1 muffin

Calories: 34

Fat: 1 g

Carbohydrate: 1 g

Protein: 6 g

Ingredients:

- ½ cup chopped baby spinach
- ¼ cup diced baby tomatoes
- ¼ cup non-fat cottage cheese
- ¼ teaspoon black pepper
- ¼ cup diced bell peppers
- 1 cup egg whites
- ¼ teaspoon kosher salt
- ¼ teaspoon garlic powder

Directions:

1. Preheat the oven to 300° F.

2. Grease a 6-count muffin pan with cooking spray.

3. Divide the spinach, tomatoes, and bell peppers equally among the muffin cups.

4. Blend egg whites, salt, cottage cheese, and seasonings until smooth.

5. Divide the egg mixture equally among the muffin cups. Stir each cup lightly.

6. Bake the muffins in the oven for 25 minutes or until they are cooked inside. The muffins will puff up while baking.

7. Cool for a few minutes before taking them out of the pan.

Crustless Egg White Quiche with Vegetables

Serves: 4

Nutritional values per serving: 1 wedge

Calories: 101

Fat: 5 g

Carbohydrate: 4.6 g

Protein: 10.1 g

Ingredients:

- Whites from 5 large eggs

- 1 clove garlic, minced

- 1 tablespoon chopped fresh herbs of your choice

- ½ cup shredded low-fat cheese of your choice

- ½ cup halved assorted cherry tomatoes

- ¼ cup 2% milk

- ⅛ cup diced onion

- Sea salt to taste

- Freshly cracked pepper to taste

- 2.5 ounces baby spinach, steamed, squeezed of extra moisture

- 2 large roasted red peppers, cut into strips

Directions:

1. Preheat the oven to 350º F.

2. Grease a small quiche pan (about 4 to 5 inches in diameter) with some cooking oil spray.

3. You can roast the red peppers on a gas stove until charred or use bottled ones.

4. Place a pan over medium heat. Spray the pan very lightly with cooking spray.

5. Add egg whites and milk into a bowl and whisk well. Stir in onion, garlic, seasonings, and herbs.

6. Spread spinach on the bottom of the quiche pan and top with red peppers and tomato slices.

7. Drizzle the egg mixture all over the vegetables in the pan. Place the pan in the oven and bake for 45 – 50 minutes or until cooked through. If you insert a toothpick in the center of the quiche and take it out, you should not find any uncooked egg stuck on it.

8. Cool for about 10 minutes. Cut into four equal wedges and serve.

Scrambled Egg Whites

Serves: 1

Calories: 135

Fat: 6 g

Carbohydrate: 7 g

Protein: 14 g

Ingredients:

- Whites of 3 large eggs

- 1 teaspoon olive oil

- ⅛ teaspoon red chili flakes

- ⅔ cup tightly packed baby spinach leaves

- 1 teaspoon grated parmesan cheese

- 1 tablespoon non-fat milk

- 1 small clove garlic

- Salt to taste

- Freshly cracked pepper to taste

- ⅔ cup cherry tomatoes, halved

- Chopped avocado to serve

Directions:

1. Beat egg whites in a bowl, adding salt, milk, and pepper until frothy.

2. Place a nonstick pan over medium heat. Add ½ teaspoon of oil and let it heat.

3. When the oil is hot, add garlic and red pepper flakes and stir for a few seconds, making sure not to burn the red pepper flakes.

4. Stir in spinach and tomatoes, and add some seasonings. Cook for a couple of minutes until the spinach has wilted, and then transfer the mixture onto a plate.

5. Add the remaining oil into the pan and let it heat. Pour the egg white mixture into the pan but do not stir until the edges begin to set slightly. Lift the edges (a little at a time) by sliding a spatula underneath the eggs and folding them over.

6. Continue doing this all around until the eggs are in a heap and are soft set, like curd. Be quick while doing so because the whites cook quickly.

7. When the eggs are soft and moist, turn off the heat. Make sure not to overcook the eggs.

8. Transfer eggs onto the plate with tomatoes. Scatter cheese on top of the eggs and serve.

Breakfast Taco

Serves: 2

Nutritional values per serving: 2 tacos

Calories: 239

Fat: 6.5 g

Carbohydrate: 23.6 g

Protein: 21.5 g

Ingredients:

- 4 corn tortillas
- 4 tablespoons shredded reduced-fat cheddar cheese
- 2 tablespoons salsa
- 1 cup liquid egg substitute

Directions:

1. Spread ½ tablespoon of salsa on each tortilla, and sprinkle with a tablespoon of cheese.

2. Place the tortillas in the microwave and heat for 30 seconds.

3. Grease a nonstick pan with cooking spray and place it over medium heat.

4. Add the egg substitute when the pan is hot and stir until cooked.

5. Add some seasonings to taste, and divide the eggs equally among the tacos. Wrap and serve.

Vegetable Skillet Frittata

Serves: 2

Nutritional values per serving: 2 wedges

Calories: 160

Fat: 5.88 g

Carbohydrate: 13.9 g

Protein: 22.49 g

Ingredients:

- 1/2 cup low-fat cottage cheese
- 2 egg whites
- 2 whole eggs
- ⅛ cup low-sodium chicken broth
- ½ cup sliced green beans
- ⅛ cup shredded carrot
- ⅛ teaspoon pepper
- ⅛ cup reduced-fat shredded cheddar cheese
- ½ cup chopped onions
- ½ cup chopped broccoli
- 1 clove garlic, minced
- ⅛ teaspoon salt or to taste

Directions:

1. Place cottage cheese, egg whites, and eggs in a blender and blend until smooth and well combined.

2. Place a nonstick pan over medium heat, add the broth, and let it heat. When the broth starts boiling, add onions and cook until onions are tender.

3. Stir in garlic, carrots, broccoli, and beans. Cover the pan and cook for a couple of minutes.

4. When the broccoli turns bright green, add salt and pepper and stir.

5. Pour the blended mixture all over the vegetables. Turn down the heat to low.

6. Continue cooking until the eggs are firm.

7. Cut into four equal wedges and serve.

Italian-Style French Toast

Serves: 2

Nutritional values per serving: 1 French toast

Calories: 372

Fat: 11.8 g

Carbohydrate: 47.1 g

Protein: 21 g

Ingredients:

- 4 tablespoons part-skim ricotta cheese

- 2 teaspoons honey

- 1 teaspoon ground cinnamon

- 2 tablespoons 1% milk

- 4 slices whole-grain bread

- 2 tablespoons sliced almonds

- 2 eggs

- ¼ cup fresh berries of your choice

Directions:

1. Spread 2 tablespoons of ricotta cheese on 2 slices of bread.

2. Trickle a teaspoon of honey on each.

3. Sprinkle a tablespoon of almonds on each, followed by a sprinkle of cinnamon.

4. Cover with the remaining 2 bread slices.

5. Beat eggs in a bowl adding milk and a bit of cinnamon.

6. Place a nonstick pan over medium heat. Spray the pan with a little cooking spray.

7. Dip the sandwiches in the egg mixture, one at a time. Make sure both sides are coated and place them in the pan. Cook until the underside is golden brown.

8. Turn the sandwiches over and cook the other side as well.

9. Place the sandwiches on individual serving plates, cut into the desired shape, place ⅛ cup of berries on each plate, and serve.

Veggie-Loaded Chickpea Waffles

Serves: 4

Nutritional values per serving: 1 waffle

Calories: 85

Fat: 4 g

Carbohydrate: 5 g

Protein: 7 g

Ingredients:

- ¼ cup chickpea flour

- ¼ cup plain 2% Greek yogurt

- 1 scallion, finely chopped

- ¼ small red pepper, very thinly sliced

- Kosher salt to taste

- Pepper to taste

- ½ cup chopped baby spinach

- 1 ½ tablespoons grated Pecorino Romano cheese

- 1/8 teaspoon baking soda

- 2 large eggs

Directions:

1. Place a wire rack over a rimmed baking sheet and place the baking sheet in the oven. Preheat oven to 200° F.

2. Set up your waffle iron and preheat it following the manufacturer's instructions.

3. Combine chickpea flour, salt, and baking soda in a bowl.

4. Add eggs and yogurt into a bowl and whisk well. Pour the yogurt mixture into a bowl of chickpea flour and whisk until smooth.

5. Stir in the scallions, red pepper, spinach, pepper, and pecorino.

6. Lightly grease the waffle iron with nonstick cooking spray.

7. Pour ¼ cup of batter per waffle into the waffle iron and cook until the waffle is golden brown or cooked as per your preference.

8. Remove the waffle from the iron and place it on the rack in the oven to keep warm.

9. Cook all the waffles similarly.

10. Serve warm.

Blueberry Protein Pancakes

Serves: 4

Nutritional values per serving: 3 pancakes, without toppings

Calories: 209

Fat: 4 g

Carbohydrate: 32 g

Protein: 11.4 g

Ingredients:

- 1 cup old-fashioned oats
- 4 egg whites
- ½ teaspoon vanilla extract
- 1 cup blueberries
- 2 eggs
- 2 medium bananas, peeled, mashed
- 1 teaspoon baking powder

Directions:

1. Place oats in the food processor bowl and grind until roughly powdered.

2. Beat eggs and egg whites in a bowl until smooth.

3. Stir in banana, baking powder, oats, and vanilla, add the blueberries and stir.

4. Place a nonstick pan over medium heat and spray it with some cooking spray.

5. Pour ¼ cup of batter into the pan for each pancake, cooking 2 to 3 at a time. Cook until the underside is browned, as per your preference. Flip the pancakes over and cook the other side as well.

6. Transfer the pancakes onto a plate and keep them warm in the oven.

7. Cook all the pancakes similarly.

8. Serve pancakes with your favorite toppings if desired.

Silky Kiwifruit Smoothie

Serves: 2

Nutritional values per serving: 1 smoothie

Calories: 200

Fat: 1 g

Carbohydrate: 31 g

Protein: 17 g

Ingredients:

- 8 ounces of light silken tofu with its liquid
- 2 cups fat-free milk
- 1 teaspoon vanilla extract
- 2 kiwifruits, peeled, sliced
- 2 teaspoon honey

Directions:

1. Place tofu, milk, vanilla, kiwifruits, and honey in a blender.
2. Blend until you get a smooth puree.
3. Pour into 2 glasses and serve with ice if desired.

Chapter 5:

Lunch Recipes

Avocado and Egg Lunch

Serves: 2

Nutritional values per serving: 1 plate

Calories: 398

Fat: 33 g

Carbohydrate: 20 g

Protein: 9 g

Ingredients:

- 2 avocados, peeled, pitted, cut each into 8 wedges

- 16 stalks baby asparagus

- Freshly ground black pepper to taste

- 2 eggs

- 2 tablespoons balsamic vinegar

Directions:

1. Preheat the oven to 350° F.

2. Brush the asparagus with a little oil and place it on a baking sheet.

3. Drizzle vinegar all over them and turn them over a few times to coat them thoroughly.

4. Place the baking sheet in the oven and bake for 5 – 7 minutes and not longer.

5. Meanwhile, boil water in a saucepan, and add a teaspoon of white vinegar if you have any.

6. Swirl the water in the pot with a spoon. Crack an egg into a bowl and carefully slide the egg into the water. Repeat with the other egg as well.

7. Cook the eggs until a film is formed on them. Remove the eggs with a slotted spoon and place them on individual serving plates.

8. Place 8 asparagus on each plate, surrounding the egg. Place avocado slices in between the asparagus.

9. Season with pepper. Drizzle some more vinegar if desired, and serve.

Lentil and Vegetable Soup

Serves: 4

Nutritional values per serving: ¼ recipe, without serving options

Calories: 96

Fat: 1 g

Carbohydrate: 22 g

Protein: 2 g

Ingredients:

- ¾ cup red lentils, rinsed, soaked in water for 30 minutes if possible

- ½ red bell pepper, chopped

- 2 large kale leaves, chopped

- ½ jalapeño, sliced (optional)

- 1 small onion, chopped

- 2 large carrots, chopped

- 1 stalk celery, chopped

- 1 russet potato, peeled, chopped

- 1 clove garlic, pressed

- ½ teaspoon dried parsley or ½ tablespoon chopped fresh parsley

- ¼ teaspoon dried oregano

- ⅛ teaspoon cayenne pepper or to taste

- ½ teaspoon salt

- ¼ teaspoon paprika

- ¼ teaspoon garlic salt

- 4 cups vegetable stock

To serve:

- Whole-grain bread

- Low-fat sour cream

Directions:

1. Place lentils in a soup pot along with the water they were soaked in. Add the vegetables, garlic, salt, spices, and stock and stir.

2. Place the pot over high heat.

3. When the soup starts boiling, turn the heat to low and simmer until the lentils and vegetables are tender.

4. If the soup is watery, boil on high for a few minutes until you get the desired thickness. You can dilute it with water or broth if it is very thick.

5. Serve with suggested serving options if desired.

Chicken Tortilla Soup with Rotisserie Chicken

Serves: 10

Nutritional values per serving: 2 cups

Calories: 339

Fat: 8 g

Carbohydrate: 26 g

Protein: 27 g

Ingredients:

- 4 cups shredded rotisserie chicken

- ⅔ cup diced onions

- 2 cans (14.5 ounces each) diced fire-roasted tomatoes

- 1 can (14 ounces) sweetcorn, drained

- 2 teaspoons Himalayan pink salt

- ½ teaspoon avocado oil

- 4 cups chicken broth

- ⅔ cup diced red peppers

- 2 cans (15 ounces each) black beans

- 2 tablespoons chili powder or to taste

- 1 teaspoon black pepper or to taste

To serve:

- 10 tablespoons cotija cheese

- ½ cup chopped cilantro

- 2 avocados, peeled, pitted, chopped

- 10 tablespoons tortilla strips

- Lime wedges

Directions:

1. Pour oil into a soup pot and let it heat over medium heat. Add onions and red bell peppers when the oil is hot and mix well.

2. Cook for a few minutes until slightly tender.

3. Mix well with the tomatoes, chicken, spices, and salt.

4. Cook for a couple of minutes, and stir in broth, corn, and black beans.

5. Let it come to a boil. Turn down the heat and let it simmer for a few minutes for the flavors to infuse.

6. Ladle into soup bowls. Divide the cheese, cilantro, avocado, and tortilla and place them in the soup bowls equally. Garnish with a lime wedge and serve.

Everything Bagel Salmon Wrap

Serves: 2

Nutritional values per serving: 1 wrap

Calories: 274

Fat: 11 g

Carbohydrate: 19 g

Protein: 24 g

Ingredients:

- 2 whole meal wraps
- 2 teaspoons of Everything Bagel seasoning
- ½ cucumber, sliced
- ⅛ cup low-fat cream cheese
- 1 can Gold Seal wild pink salmon
- ½ bell pepper, sliced

Directions:

1. Spread a tablespoon of cream cheese on each wrap. Scatter Everything Bagel seasoning all over.

2. Mash salmon and divide it equally among the wraps, spreading it on them.

3. Place cucumber and bell pepper slices on top. Wrap and serve.

Thai Prawn Mango Salad

Serves: 2

Nutritional values per serving: ½ recipe

Calories: 383

Fat: 2 g

Carbohydrate: 73 g

Protein: 18 g

Ingredients:

- 7 ounces large prawns, shelled, deveined
- ¾ tablespoon fish sauce
- ½ tablespoon grated ginger
- 1 Thai red chili or green chili, finely chopped
- 1 teaspoon salt divided
- 1 tablespoon lime juice or white vinegar
- ¾ tablespoon coconut sugar or brown sugar
- 2 cloves garlic, minced
- ½ English cucumber, cut into 1-inch pieces
- ½ ripe mango, cut into 1-inch cubes
- 3 tablespoons chopped cilantro stem and leaves
- 3 tablespoons chopped mint leaves

- ½ onion, halved; separate the layers

- ¼ cup sliced red or yellow bell pepper

- 3 tablespoons chopped basil leaves

- ½ cup cooked rice vermicelli noodles

Directions:

1. Boil a pot of water with ½ teaspoon of salt over high heat. When the water starts boiling, add the prawns. Cook for 1 ½ - 2 minutes if the prawns are large or for about 30 seconds if the prawns are small in size. Either way, cook them until they start curling, and they will also turn a bit pink in color.

2. Drain and rinse under cold running water. Drain well.

3. To make the dressing: Add lime juice, sugar, garlic, remaining salt, fish sauce, ginger, and chilies into a bowl. Stir until sugar dissolves completely. Cover and keep it in the refrigerator until you serve the salad.

4. To make the salad: Combine prawns, onion, cucumber, and mango in a bowl.

5. Pour half the dressing over and mix well.

6. To assemble: Divide the vermicelli noodles equally between two plates and top each with the remaining noodles.

7. Place salad on top and serve.

Avocado Egg Salad

Serves: 1

Calories: 192

Fat: 14 g

Carbohydrate: 3.4 g

Protein: 13.2 g

Ingredients:

- ¼ cup mashed ripe avocado

- ¼ teaspoon kosher salt

- 2 hard-boiled eggs, peeled, finely chopped

- 1 teaspoon fresh lemon juice

- ½ teaspoon chopped chives

Directions:

1. Add avocado, salt, lemon juice, and chives into a bowl and stir.

2. Stir in the eggs and serve.

Strawberry Chicken Salad

Serves: 2

Nutritional values per serving: ½ recipe

Calories: 92

Fat: 1 g

Carbohydrate: 8 g

Protein: 14 g

Ingredients:

- 3 ounces grilled chicken breast strips

- ½ cup sliced fresh strawberries

- 2 tablespoons low-sodium chicken broth

- ½ teaspoon honey mustard

- A dash of ground black pepper

- ½ cup diced cucumber

- 1 teaspoon chopped fresh mint

- ½ tablespoon rice wine vinegar

- A dash of salt

- 2 cups baby spinach leaves

Directions:

1. Add chicken, strawberries, cucumber, and mint into a bowl and stir.

2. To make the dressing: Add broth, honey, vinegar, salt, and pepper to a small jar. Fasten the lid and shake vigorously for a few seconds until well combined.

3. Pour the dressing over the salad. Toss well.

4. Place a cup of spinach leaves on each serving plate, divide the salad equally, and place it over the spinach.

5. Serve.

BBQ Chicken Salad

Serves: 2

Nutritional values per serving: ½ recipe

Calories: 376

Fat: 24 g

Carbohydrate: 21 g

Protein: 18 g

Ingredients:

For cilantro ranch dressing:

- ¼ teaspoon dried dill

- ¼ teaspoon garlic powder

- ⅛ teaspoon fine sea salt

- ¼ teaspoon dried parsley

- ¼ teaspoon onion powder

- ⅛ teaspoon ground black pepper

- ¼ cup low-fat Greek yogurt

- ½ tablespoon lemon juice

- ½ - 1 tablespoon unsweetened almond milk

- ¼ cup fresh cilantro leaves

For the salad:

- ½ pound baked BBQ chicken breast or leftover shredded grilled / rotisserie chicken, diced

- 2 – 3 cups lettuce leaves

- ½ cup chopped tomatoes

- ½ cup cooked or canned black beans, rinsed

- 2 tablespoons BBQ sauce

- ¼ small red onion, diced

- ½ cup thawed, frozen corn kernels

Directions:

1. To make the dressing: Blend seasonings, yogurt, lemon juice, almond milk, and cilantro until smooth.

2. You can get the recipe for BBQ chicken under the chapter, Dinner Recipes.

3. Combine chicken and BBQ sauce in a bowl.

4. To make the salad: Take 2 bowls and distribute the lettuce, tomatoes, onions, corn, and black beans among the bowls.

5. Put the chicken on top, pour the required amount of cilantro dressing on top and serve. You may not require all the dressing add according to your taste.

Chicken Salad Stuffed Avocados

Serves: 2

Nutritional values per serving: 1 stuffed avocado half

Calories: 309

Fat: 20 g

Carbohydrate: 14 g

Protein: 22 g

Ingredients:

- 1 cup shredded rotisserie chicken

- 1 large avocado, halved, pitted

- Juice of ½ lemon

- Kosher salt to taste

- Freshly ground pepper to taste

- Red pepper flakes to garnish

- ½ small red onion, finely chopped

- 3 tablespoons plain low-fat Greek yogurt

- ½ tablespoon Dijon mustard

- 1 tablespoon chopped parsley plus extra to garnish

Directions:

1. With a spoon, remove some of the avocado pulp surrounding the pit area, leaving the pulp intact near the skin. You need to have scooped-out avocado shells.

2. Chop the pulp into small pieces.

3. Combine chopped avocado, chicken, yogurt, lemon juice, onion, parsley, and Dijon mustard in a bowl. Add salt and pepper to taste.

4. Distribute the salad equally and fill the avocado halves. Sprinkle parsley, red pepper flakes, and black pepper on top, and serve.

Cucumber Sandwich

Serves: 2

Nutritional values per serving: 1 sandwich

Calories: 358

Fat: 22 g

Carbohydrate: 29 g

Protein: 12 g

Ingredients:

- 4 ounces of low-fat cream cheese at room temperature

- 2 tablespoons thinly sliced chives

- ½ teaspoon ground pepper

- ⅔ cup thinly sliced English cucumber

- 2 tablespoons low-fat plain Greek yogurt

- 2 tablespoons chopped fresh dill

- 4 slices whole wheat sandwich bread

Directions:

1. Add cream cheese, chives, pepper, yogurt, and dill into a small bowl and stir until smooth.

2. Divide the cream cheese mixture and spread it on top of each bread slice.

3. Place 1/3 cup of cucumber slices on two slices of bread.

4. Cover with the remaining bread slices, with the cream cheese side facing down.

5. Cut into the desired shape and serve.

Turkey Apple Burgers

Serves: 2

Nutritional values per serving: 1 burger

Calories: 197

Fat: 5 g

Carbohydrate: 13 g

Protein: 27 g

Ingredients:

- 1 green apple, cored, peeled, halved
- ½ tablespoon minced fresh sage or thyme
- ¼ teaspoon salt
- ⅛ teaspoon garlic powder
- 1 teaspoon olive oil
- ½ pound 99% lean ground turkey
- 1 teaspoon Dijon mustard
- ⅛ teaspoon ground black pepper
- ⅛ teaspoon onion powder

Directions:

1. Thinly slice half the apple and grate the other half.

2. Combine grated apple, seasonings, and turkey in a bowl.

3. Divide the mixture into 2 equal parts and shape each part into a patty.

4. Place a nonstick pan over medium heat. Brush oil on either side of the patties and place in the pan. Cook until brown on each side and cooked through inside.

5. Place a burger on each serving plate. Divide the sliced apple equally and place it on top of the burger.

6. Serve.

Beef-Stuffed Peppers

Serves: 2

Nutritional values per serving: 1 stuffed pepper

Calories: 278

Fat: 7.21 g

Carbohydrate: 26.96 g

Protein: 28.3 g

Ingredients:

- ½ pound 93% lean or leaner ground beef
- ¼ cup minced onion
- ½ can (from 14.5 ounces can) diced tomatoes with green peppers and onions, drained
- 1 ½ tablespoons tomato paste
- ¼ teaspoon salt
- Chopped fresh parsley to garnish
- 2 medium bell peppers of any color (you can use assorted)
- 1 teaspoon minced garlic
- ¼ cup cooked brown rice
- 1 teaspoon dried parsley
- ⅛ teaspoon pepper

Directions:

1. Preheat the oven to 475° F.

2. Grease a baking dish with a little cooking spray.

3. Cut off a slice (near the stem) from each bell pepper. Do not discard the tops, these will be used as a lid.

4. Gently remove any seeds and membranes from the bell peppers with a paring knife.

5. Place the bell peppers upright in the baking dish and put the 'lids' on them. Cover the dish with foil.

6. Place the baking dish in the oven and set the timer for 15 minutes.

7. Take the baking dish from the oven and let it cool for 5 – 10 minutes.

8. In the meantime, place a nonstick pan over medium heat. Add onion, beef, and garlic when the pan is hot and stir. As you stir, crumble the meat into smaller pieces.

9. Stir on and off for about 3 minutes. Add tomatoes, tomato paste, salt, parsley, pepper, and rice, and mix well. Heat thoroughly and turn off the heat.

10. Now, fill the bell peppers with the mixture. Place the tops of the bell peppers back on the bell peppers, and put the baking dish into the oven.

11. Cook until the internal temperature of the meat stuffing shows 160° F on the meat thermometer.

12. Sprinkle parsley on top and serve.

Shrimp Garden Salad

Serves: 3

Nutritional values per serving: ½ recipe, without dressing

Calories: 73

Fat: 1 g

Carbohydrate: 10 g

Protein: 8 g

Ingredients:

- ½ head Romaine lettuce, chopped
- ½ bunch of green onions, chopped
- 2 medium tomatoes, chopped
- ½ can (from 4.5 ounces can) of small shrimp, drained
- 1 bunch of radishes, sliced
- ½ cucumber, peeled and chopped
- 1 ½ ribs celery, chopped
- Seasonings of your choice
- Dressing of your choice (optional)

Directions:

1. Combine shrimp, vegetables, and seasonings in a bowl. Add dressing if using and toss well.
2. Serve.

Veggie and Hummus Sandwich

Serves: 2

Nutritional values per serving: 1 sandwich

Calories: 325

Fat: 14.3 g

Carbohydrate: 39.7 g

Protein: 12.8 g

Ingredients:

- 4 slices whole-grain bread

- ½ avocado, peeled, mashed

- ½ medium red bell pepper, sliced

- ½ cup shredded carrot

- 6 tablespoons hummus

- 1 cup mixed salad greens

- ½ cup sliced cucumber

Directions:

1. Spread 3 tablespoons of hummus on 2 slices of bread.

2. Divide the salad greens, cucumber, bell pepper, and carrots equally and place them over the hummus in layers.

3. Divide the avocado equally and spread it on the other 2 bread slices.

4. Cover the sandwiches with the avocado spread bread slices, with the avocado side facing down.

5. Cut into the desired shape and serve.

Mediterranean Tuna and Spinach Salad

Serves: 2

Nutritional values per serving: 1 cup tuna salad with 2 cups spinach and an orange

Calories: 376

Fat: 21 g

Carbohydrate: 26.2 g

Protein: 25.7 g

Ingredients:

- 3 tablespoons tahini
- 3 tablespoons water
- 8 kalamata olives, pitted, chopped
- ¼ cup chopped parsley
- 2 medium oranges, peeled
- 3 tablespoons lemon juice
- 2 cans (5 ounces each) of light tuna chunks in water, drained
- ¼ cup feta cheese
- 4 cups baby spinach

Directions:

1. To make the salad: Combine tahini, water, and lemon juice in a bowl. Stir in olives, tuna, feta, and parsley, and add some seasonings to taste if desired.

2. Place 2 cups of spinach on each plate. Divide the salad among the plates and spread it over the spinach. Place an orange on each plate and serve.

Fabulous Flatbread Pizzas

Serves: 1

Calories: 333

Fat: 12 g

Carbohydrate: 42 g

Protein: 18 g

Ingredients:

- ½ beetroot, cooked, thinly sliced

- 1 radish, thinly sliced

- 1 tablespoon hummus

- 1-ounce low-fat feta cheese

- 1/22 tablespoon sunflower seeds

- ½ spring onion, sliced

- ½ small tomato, thinly sliced

- 1 small flatbread

- ½ tablespoon chopped fresh basil

For the dip:

- ¼ cucumber, grated

- ½ cup plain nonfat or soy yogurt

- ⅛ cup fresh herbs of your choice, chopped

- Salt to taste

- Pepper to taste

Directions:

1. Preheat the oven to 350° F. Place the flatbread on a baking sheet.

2. Smear hummus over the flatbread, and top with beetroot slices, radish slices, followed by tomatoes and spring onions.

3. Scatter feta cheese and, finally, sunflower seeds.

4. Place the baking sheet in the oven and set the timer for 8 to 9 minutes.

5. Garnish with fresh herbs and serve.

Southwestern Veggie Wraps

Serves: 3

Nutritional values per serving: 1 wrap

Calories: 295

Fat: 4 g

Carbohydrate: 53 g

Protein: 11 g

Ingredients:

- ½ can (from a 15-ounce can) of black beans, rinsed, drained
- ½ cup frozen corn, thawed
- 3 tablespoons fat-free sour cream
- 1 shallot, chopped
- 1 tablespoon lime juice
- ¼ teaspoon chili powder
- 3 Romaine lettuce leaves
- 1 large tomato, deseeded, diced
- ½ cup cooked brown rice, cooled
- ⅛ cup minced fresh cilantro
- ½ jalapeño pepper, deseeded, chopped
- ¼ teaspoon ground cumin

- ¼ teaspoon salt

- 3 whole-wheat tortillas (8 inches each) at room temperature

Directions:

1. Place beans, corn, sour cream, shallot, lime juice, chili powder, tomato, rice, cilantro, jalapeño, cumin, and salt in a bowl and mix until well combined.

2. Divide the bean mixture equally among the tortillas and roll them tightly. Fasten with toothpicks if required.

3. Cut into two halves if desired and serve.

Salmon Bean Wraps

Serves: 4

Nutritional values per serving: 1 wrap

Calories: 315

Fat: 7 g

Carbohydrate: 44 g

Protein: 16 g

Ingredients:

- ½ cup peeled, mashed avocado
- ½ cup finely chopped tomato
- 6 tablespoons fat-free sour cream
- 3 teaspoons lemon juice
- 4 whole-wheat tortillas (8 inches each) at room temperature
- 2 cups shredded lettuce
- 1 ½ cups canned or cooked black beans, rinsed, drained
- 6 tablespoons minced fresh cilantro
- ¼ cup finely chopped onion
- ½ teaspoon pepper or to taste
- 4 ounces flaked, smoked salmon filets

Directions:

1. Add avocado, tomato, sour cream, lemon juice, beans, cilantro, onion, and pepper in a bowl.

2. Keep the bowl covered in the refrigerator for 30 – 60 minutes.

3. Place ¾ cup of the mixture over each tortilla and spread it evenly. Place 1 ounce of salmon on each tortilla, followed by ½ cup of lettuce.

4. Wrap tightly and fasten with toothpicks.

5. Cut into 2 halves if desired and serve.

Chapter 6:

Heavy Dishes Ideal for Family Get Togethers

Vegan 'Fesenjan' with Roasted Butternut Squash and Brown Rice Pilaf

Serves: 8

Nutritional values per serving: 1/8 recipe

Calories: 503

Fat: 15.25 g

Carbohydrate: 90.18 g

Protein: 8.76 g

Ingredients:

For Fesenjan:

- 2 heaping cups of walnuts or almonds, lightly toasted, cooled

- 10 Medjool dates, pitted

- 1 1/3 cups low-sodium vegetable broth

- 2/3 cup pomegranate syrup/molasses

- 1 teaspoon saffron dissolved in ½ cup water

- 2 medium onions, finely chopped

- 2 large butternut squashes, halved lengthwise

- 2 teaspoons ground cinnamon

- 1 teaspoon olive oil

- 1 ½ cups water

For rice pilaf:

- 4 teaspoons sumac

- 8 large cloves garlic, sliced

- 2 cups brown rice, rinsed and soaked in water for an hour

- Zest of 4 lemons, grated

Directions:

1. Preheat oven to 375° F.

2. Scoop out the center of the squash halves, cut each half into large semi-circular slices, and place them on a baking sheet.

3. Brush squash slices lightly using 1 teaspoon of oil and season with salt and pepper.

4. Place the baking sheet in the oven and cook for about 20 to 30 minutes or until the squash is tender.

5. Cook the rice following the directions given on the package, then add the sumac and cover the pan.

6. To make Fesenjan sauce: Add walnuts into a blender and blend until finely chopped.

7. Place a large pot over medium-high heat, and spray with a little cooking spray. Add onions, stir and cook until it turns pink.

8. Add walnuts and water and stir. When it begins to boil, reduce the heat to low and simmer for about 15 minutes.

9. In the meantime, add about ½ cup pomegranate syrup, broth, and dates into a blender and blend until smooth.

10. Pour into the simmering broth. Add the saffron, salt, pepper, and cinnamon.

11. Taste the sauce and add the remaining pomegranate syrup if required. Add more water to dilute the sauce if desired.

12. Place a lid on the pot and simmer for 30-40 minutes or until thick, stirring occasionally. Turn off the heat.

13. Serve 1/8 recipe of rice on each plate. Place 1/8 of the squash slices over the rice on each plate, and spoon 1/8 of the Fesenjan sauce on top and serve.

Garden-Stuffed Zucchini Boats

Serves: 6

Nutritional values per serving: 2 boats

Calories: 489

Fat: 24 g

Carbohydrate: 28 g

Protein: 36 g

Ingredients:

- 6 medium zucchini, trimmed, halved lengthwise

- 1 ½ cups chopped onions

- 4 cloves garlic, minced

- 1 ½ cups canned fire-roasted diced tomatoes or chopped fresh tomatoes with its liquid

- ⅔ cup chopped fresh mushrooms

- 4 teaspoons minced fresh thyme or 2 teaspoons dried thyme

- ½ teaspoon salt

- ½ cup grated parmesan cheese

- Pasta sauce to serve (optional)

- 1 ½ pounds of ground beef

- 1 cup chopped green pepper

- 3 cups water divided

- 1 cup roasted red sweet peppers

- ½ cup uncooked ditalini or any other small pasta

- 1 teaspoon minced fresh oregano or ½ teaspoon dried oregano

- ½ teaspoon pepper

- 2 cups shredded Italian cheese blend, divided

Directions:

1. Preheat the oven to 350° F.

2. Place the zucchini halves in a baking dish so the cut side faces down.

3. Place the baking dish in the oven and set the timer for 10 minutes.

4. Take out the baking sheet and let the zucchini cool for a while. Remove the seeds with a spoon, leaving the skin and a little pulp (about ¼ inch) near the skin intact. These zucchini shells will be the boats.

5. In the meantime, place a skillet over medium heat. Add onion, garlic, beef, and green pepper and stir, breaking the meat into smaller pieces. Cook until the meat is not pink anymore. Drain off any fat from the pan.

6. Add about 2 cups of water into the pan along with red peppers, pasta, tomatoes, mushrooms, herbs, and seasonings, and stir.

7. Stir on and off until the pasta cooks, and the mixture is thick. Add Parmesan cheese and stir, then turn the heat off.

8. Divide the mixture equally between the zucchini shells.

9. Place the zucchini shells back in the baking dish and scatter 1-½ cups of Italian cheese blend on top of the stuffing. Pour a cup of water around the zucchini boats into the baking dish.

10. Cover the baking dish with foil and place it in the oven. Set the timer for 25 minutes.

11. After baking for 20 minutes, remove the foil and top with the remaining Italian cheese blend. Continue baking for the remaining time or until the cheese melts.

12. Drizzle some pasta sauce on top if using, and serve.

Lentil Burgers

Serves: 8

Nutritional values per serving: 1 burger, without serving options

Calories: 317

Fat: 8 g

Carbohydrate: 45 g

Protein: 18 g

Ingredients:

- 3 cups dried red lentils, rinsed, soaked in water for 2 hours, drained

- 2 large shallots or 2 small onions, finely chopped

- 2 tablespoons tomato paste

- 2 teaspoons salt or to taste

- 4 large cloves garlic, peeled, minced

- ⅔ cup grated carrots

- ½ cup chopped cilantro

- 1 teaspoon pepper

To serve: Optional

- Whole wheat burger buns

- Salad

- Roasted potatoes

- Roasted sweet potatoes

- Any other side dish of your choice

Directions:

1. Preheat the oven to 400° F. Place a sheet of parchment paper on a large baking sheet.

2. Place lentils, shallots, tomato paste, pepper, salt, cilantro, carrot, and garlic in the food processor bowl.

3. Give short pulses until well incorporated, and the mixture sticks together when you press some of it in your fist.

4. Divide the mixture into 8 equal portions. Shape each into a patty and place on the prepared baking sheet.

5. Place the baking sheet in the oven and set the timer for 20 minutes until brown and crisp. Flip the patties after about 10 – 12 minutes of baking.

6. Serve hot.

Chickpea and Quinoa Grain Bowl

Serves: 2

Nutritional values per serving: 1 bowl

Calories: 503

Fat: 16.6 g

Carbohydrate: 75 g

Protein: 17.9 g

Ingredients:

- 2 cups cooked quinoa
- 1 cup cucumber slices
- ½ avocado, peeled, pitted, and diced
- 2 tablespoons finely chopped roasted red peppers
- ⅛ cup water + extra if desired
- ¼ teaspoon salt
- ⅔ cup cooked or canned chickpeas, rinsed, drained
- 1 cup cherry tomatoes, halved
- 6 tablespoons hummus
- 2 tablespoons lemon juice
- 2 teaspoons chopped fresh parsley (optional)
- ¼ teaspoon pepper or to taste

Directions:

1. Place a cup of quinoa in each bowl and layer with 1/3 cup chickpeas, followed by ½ cup cucumber and ½ cup tomatoes. Finally, divide the avocado among the bowls.

2. To make the dressing: Whisk together hummus, lemon juice, water, roasted red pepper, parsley, pepper, and salt in a bowl.

3. Drizzle an equal quantity of dressing in each bowl and serve.

Chicken and Vegetable Noodle Soup

Serves: 3

Nutritional values per serving: 2 cups

Calories: 256

Fat: 4.8 g

Carbohydrate: 29 g

Protein: 23.7 g

Ingredients:

- ½ pound boneless, skinless chicken breast
- 2 cups low-sodium chicken broth
- ½ cup chopped orange bell pepper
- ½ tablespoon Italian seasoning
- ⅛ teaspoon salt or to taste
- 2 small bay leaves
- 1 tablespoon chopped fresh basil
- ¼ cup grated parmesan cheese
- ½ can (from 14 ounces can) of unsalted fire-roasted diced tomatoes
- ¾ cup chopped yellow onion
- 2 cloves garlic, peeled, minced
- ¼ teaspoon pepper or to taste

- ⅛ teaspoon crushed red pepper

- 3 ounces whole-wheat rotini pasta

- 1 tablespoon chopped fresh flat-leaf parsley plus extra to garnish

Directions:

1. Add tomatoes, chicken, onion, garlic, broth, seasonings, bay leaves, and broth into a soup pot.

2. Place the pot over high heat. When the mixture starts boiling, turn down the heat and cook covered until the chicken is cooked through - the internal temperature in the thickest part of the meat should show 165° F on the meat thermometer.

3. Pick the bay leaves out and discard them. Remove the chicken from the pot and place it on your cutting board. Let it cool for a while.

4. Add pasta to the soup pot and stir. Continue cooking covered over medium-high heat until pasta is al dente, stirring occasionally.

5. Shred or chop the chicken and add it to the soup pot. Stir in basil and parsley and heat thoroughly.

6. Ladle into soup bowls and serve garnished with some parsley.

Low-Calorie Pasta

Serves: 8

Nutritional values per serving: ⅛ recipe

Calories: 196

Fat: 3 g

Carbohydrate: 29 g

Protein: 28 g

Ingredients:

For the pasta:

- 6 cups cooked low-calorie pasta like Fiber Gourmet light pasta

- 4 cups fat-free mozzarella cheese divided

- 2 tablespoons Italian seasonings

- 2 cups fat-free cottage cheese

- 2 large eggs

For pasta sauce:

- 3 cups tomato sauce or passata

- 1 teaspoon salt

- 2 teaspoons brown sugar substitute

- 2 teaspoons Italian seasonings

- 1 teaspoon pepper

Directions:

1. Preheat the oven to 350° F. Prepare a baking dish (13 x 9 inches) by greasing it with cooking spray.

2. Follow the directions given on the package to cook the pasta. For 6 cups of cooked pasta, you may need around 2 ½ - 3 cups of uncooked pasta.

3. To make pasta sauce: Whisk together tomato sauce, seasonings, and brown sugar substitute in a bowl.

4. Combine cottage cheese, eggs, 2 cups mozzarella, cottage cheese, Italian herbs, and half the sauce mixture in a bowl.

5. Stir in the pasta.

6. To assemble: Spread about ½ cup of sauce on the bottom of the baking dish.

7. Spread the pasta mixture into the baking dish. Spoon the remaining sauce mixture over the pasta.

8. Scatter the remaining mozzarella cheese on the sauce layer. Cover the dish with foil and place it in the oven, and set the timer for 35 – 40 minutes. Remove the foil and continue baking for a few more minutes until the cheese melts and is brown at a few spots.

Vegan Jambalaya

Serves: 3

Nutritional values per serving: 1/3 recipe

Calories: 358

Fat: 1.9 g

Carbohydrate: 74 g

Protein: 15.4 g

Ingredients:

- 2 tablespoons water

- 2 cloves garlic, minced

- 1 large rib of celery, diced

- ½ teaspoon dried thyme

- ½ teaspoon dried oregano

- ½ can (from 14 ounces can) of crushed tomatoes

- 1 bay leaf

- ½ can (from a 15-ounce can) of red kidney beans, rinsed, drained

- ½ teaspoon pink salt or to taste

- ½ medium onion, diced

- ½ large green bell pepper, deseeded, diced

- ½ large red bell pepper, deseeded, diced

- ½ large yellow bell pepper, deseeded, diced

- 1 teaspoon smoked paprika

- ⅛ teaspoon cayenne pepper or red pepper flakes

- ¾ cup long grain brown rice, rinsed, soaked in water for an hour, drained

- 2 cups low-sodium vegetable broth or more if required

- 1 ½ - 2 vegan sausages (about 7 – 8 ounces), sliced or extra ½ can beans

- ½ tablespoon cooking oil (to be used only for sausages)

- Freshly cracked pepper to taste

To serve:

- Thinly sliced scallions or green onions

- Hot sauce to taste

- Chopped parsley

Directions:

1. If you are using vegan sausage, it needs to be cooked. Place a pan over medium heat, add oil and swirl the pan to spread it.

2. Place sausage slices in the pan and cook until brown on each side.

3. Remove the sausage slices from the pan and place them on layers of paper napkins.

4. Now add water to the pan. Add onion, celery, garlic, and bell

114

peppers when the water is hot and stir. Cook for a few minutes until the water has nearly evaporated.

5. Stir in the spices. Keep stirring for about a minute until you get a nice aroma, but do not burn them.

6. Stir in the bay leaf, rice, tomatoes, and broth. When the mixture starts boiling, turn the heat to low and cook covered until the rice is tender. Make sure to stir on and off.

7. Stir in the kidney beans and sausages. Heat thoroughly.

8. Discard the bay leaf. Add salt and pepper and stir.

9. Serve in bowls garnished with scallions, parsley, and hot sauce.

Chapter 7:

Dinner Recipes

BBQ Chicken Breast

Serves: 2

Nutritional values per serving: ½ recipe, without side dish

Calories: 550

Fat: 16 g

Carbohydrate: 28 g

Protein: 70 g

Ingredients:

- 1 pound boneless, skinless chicken breasts
- 1 teaspoon coconut sugar
- ½ teaspoon onion powder
- ¼ teaspoon paprika
- Cayenne pepper to taste
- ½ tablespoon apple cider vinegar
- ½ teaspoon garlic powder
- ½ teaspoon salt
- ¼ teaspoon chili powder

- ¼ cup BBQ sauce

Directions:

1. Preheat the oven to 400° F.

2. Place a sheet of parchment paper or cling wrap over your countertop and lay the chicken breasts over it. Place another sheet of parchment paper on top and pound the chicken with a meat mallet until it is uniformly 1 inch thick.

3. Remove the parchment paper and discard it. Put the chicken into a baking dish.

4. Drizzle vinegar all over the chicken.

5. Combine sugar, salt, and spices in a bowl and rub it all over the chicken.

6. Prick the chicken with a fork in several places. Cover the dish and let it rest for 30 minutes.

7. Drizzle BBQ sauce all over the chicken. Place the baking dish in the oven and set the timer for 30 minutes or bake until the internal temperature of the chicken shows 155° F to 160° F on the meat thermometer.

8. Take out the baking dish and tent it loosely with foil. After resting it for about 10 minutes, cut it into slices and serve it with a side dish of your choice.

Middle Eastern Chicken Stew with Lentils and Spinach

Serves: 3

Nutritional values per serving: 1/3 recipe without serving options

Calories: 312

Fat: 4.6 g

Carbohydrate: 23.6 g

Protein: 43.6 g

Ingredients:

- 1 pound boneless, skinless chicken breasts cut into 1-inch chunks

- 2 medium carrots, chopped

- 6 tablespoons brown or green lentils, rinsed, soaked in water for 2 hours

- 1 tablespoon tomato paste

- Juice of ½ lemon

- ½ package (from a 10 ounces package) of frozen chopped spinach, thawed, squeezed of excess moisture

- ½ onion, chopped

- 1 ½ cups low-sodium chicken broth

- ¼ teaspoon garlic powder

- Salt to taste

- Pepper to taste

To serve: Optional

- Cooked brown or white rice

- Cauliflower rice

- Crusty bread

Directions:

1. Combine chicken, vegetables, lentils, tomato paste, broth, and garlic powder in a soup pot over medium heat. If you have an instant pot, you can cook the stew in it. It is much quicker.

2. When the soup starts boiling, turn the heat low and cook covered until the lentils are tender and the stew is thick.

3. Stir on and off. Add lemon juice, salt, and pepper and stir.

4. Ladle into bowls and serve with any of the suggested serving options.

Salsa Chicken

Serves: 3

Nutritional values per serving: 1/3 recipe, without serving options

Calories: 324

Fat: 2.9 g

Carbohydrate: 36.7 g

Protein: 42 g

Ingredients:

- 1 ½ cups frozen corn kernels

- ½ can (from 15 ounces can) of petite diced tomatoes

- ½ teaspoon minced garlic

- 1 pound boneless, skinless chicken breasts

- ½ can (from a 15-ounce can) of black beans, drained, rinsed

- ½ cup salsa, divided

- Pepper to taste

- ¼ teaspoon ground cumin

- Salt to taste

Directions:

1. Preheat the oven to 375° F. Coat a baking dish with a little cooking spray.

2. Add corn, tomatoes, garlic, black beans, ¼ cup salsa, and cumin into the baking dish and stir.

3. Spread the chicken over the mixture, and sprinkle it with salt and pepper.

4. Spread the remaining salsa over the chicken.

5. Cover the dish with foil and place it in the oven. Set the timer for 45 to 50 minutes or cook until the internal temperature of the meat in the thickest part shows 165° F on the meat thermometer.

6. Take the chicken from the dish and slice it. Add it back into the dish and mix well.

7. Serve as desired.

8. You can serve the chicken in tacos, place it as a filling in quesadillas, or add it to a salad. You can also make it into burritos or burrito bowls, adding cooked brown rice, quinoa, or any other grains of your choice along with toppings.

9. If you are using it in quesadillas, after slicing the chicken, do not mix it with the ingredients in the baking dish. Simply place the filling over the tortillas with a sprinkle of cheese. Cover with another tortilla and cook in a pan or oven until crisp. Use the baking dish's bean mixture as a quesadilla dip.

Garden Chicken Cacciatore

Serves: 6

Nutritional values per serving: 3 ounces cooked chicken with ½ cup sauce

Calories: 207

Fat: 9 g

Carbohydrate: 8 g

Protein: 23 g

Ingredients:

- 6 boneless, skinless chicken thighs
- ½ can (from 14.5 ounces can) of diced tomatoes with oregano, basil, and garlic with its liquid
- ½ medium onion, chopped
- ⅛ cup red wine or extra chicken broth
- Salt to taste
- 1 tablespoon cornstarch mixed with 1 tablespoon water
- Minced fresh parsley to garnish
- 1 medium green bell pepper, chopped
- 3 ounces tomato paste
- ¼ cup low-sodium chicken broth
- 2 cloves garlic, peeled, minced

- A pinch pepper

Directions:

1. Add bell peppers, tomato paste, broth, garlic, pepper, tomatoes, onion, garlic, and pepper into a heavy pan or Dutch oven.

2. Stir well and add in the chicken. Give it a good stir and cover the pan.

3. Place the pan over medium heat. When the mixture starts boiling, reduce the heat to low and simmer until the chicken is cooked.

4. Stir in the cornstarch mixture. Keep stirring until thick.

5. Garnish with parsley and serve.

Chicken with Spinach and Mushrooms

Serves: 2

Nutritional values per serving: ½ recipe

Calories: 406

Fat: 11.01 g

Carbohydrate: 6.68 g

Protein: 67.38 g

Ingredients:

- 2 skinless, boneless chicken breast halves cut into 1-inch pieces

- Ground black pepper to taste

- ½ can (from a 15-ounce can) of diced tomatoes, drained

- 1 cup thinly sliced mushrooms

- Salt to taste

- 1 clove garlic, peeled, minced

- 2.5 ounces of baby spinach

- ¼ cup grated parmesan cheese

Directions:

1. Sprinkle salt and pepper all over the chicken.

2. Place a nonstick pan over medium heat and spray it with a little cooking spray.

3. When the pan heats, place the chicken in it and cook until it is not pink anymore.

4. Transfer the chicken onto a plate, cover and leave it aside for now.

5. To the same pan, add garlic and cook for about a minute or until you get a nice aroma.

6. Stir in the tomatoes, mushrooms, and spinach. Cook until it is thickened, as per your preference.

7. Stir in the chicken. Taste the gravy and add more salt and pepper if required.

8. Garnish with cheese and serve.

Turkey Soup

Serves: 4

Nutritional values per serving: ¼ recipe

Calories: 364

Fat: 3 g

Carbohydrate: 48 g

Protein: 40 g

Ingredients:

- ½ pound ground turkey

- ½ can (from a 14.5-ounce can) of diced tomatoes

- 1 ½ cups mixed vegetables of your choice

- 1 cup vegetable broth

- 12 ounces pasta sauce

- ½ can (from a 15.5 ounce can) of black beans, drained, rinsed

- Pepper to taste

- ½ teaspoon dried Italian herbs

- Salt to taste

Directions:

1. Place a nonstick pan over medium heat. Add turkey and cook until brown, stirring to break the meat into crumbles. Take the pan off the heat.

2. Transfer the meat to a soup pot over medium heat.

3. Stir in the vegetables, tomatoes, broth, pasta sauce, black beans, herbs, and seasonings. Let it come to a boil.

4. Cover the pot and simmer for about 15 – 20 minutes.

5. Stir occasionally. Ladle into soup bowls and serve.

Asian Meatballs with Cucumber and Carrot Slaw

Serves: 2

Nutritional values per serving: ½ recipe, without sesame oil

Calories: 234

Fat: 7.49 g

Carbohydrate: 14.64 g

Protein: 27.15 g

Ingredients:

- ½ medium cucumber, shredded

- 1 ½ water chestnuts, finely chopped

- ½ medium carrot, shredded

- 1 tablespoon low-sodium soy sauce

- ⅛ teaspoon ground pepper

- ½ pound ground lean pork

- ½ tablespoon finely chopped scallions

- 1 large egg

- ⅛ cup panko breadcrumbs

- ½ teaspoon sesame oil (optional)

Directions:

1. To make the slaw: Add carrot and cucumber into a bowl and stir. Cover and set aside until ready to serve.

2. Preheat the oven to 375° F.

3. Place pork, scallion, egg, breadcrumbs, water chestnut, soy sauce, and pepper in the food processor bowl and give a few short pulses until well combined.

4. Make the mixture into meatballs and put them on a baking sheet.

5. Set the timer for 10 – 12 minutes or until the meatballs are not pink anymore and clear juices are released. Turn the meatballs over after about 6 – 7 minutes of baking.

6. To make the sauce: Whisk together soy sauce, ginger, scallion, and sesame oil, if using, in a bowl. Sesame oil will give you an authentic Asian flavor.

7. To assemble: Place the slaw on the center of a serving platter in a heap. Surround the vegetables with meatballs. Trickle sauce over the meatballs and serve.

Taco Stuffed Sweet Potatoes

Serves: 2

Nutritional values per serving: 2 stuffed sweet potato halves without toppings

Calories: 493

Fat: 6 g

Carbohydrate: 80 g

Protein: 31 g

Ingredients:

- ½ pound lean ground beef
- 1 clove garlic, peeled, minced
- ½ cup chunky salsa
- 2 medium sweet potatoes (12 – 14 ounces each)
- ½ medium onion, chopped
- ½ packet taco seasoning or to taste
- ⅛ – ¼ cup water

Toppings: Optional

- Diced tomatoes
- Shredded Mexican blend cheese
- Guacamole
- Diced avocado
- Salsa

- Fat-free sour cream

- Chopped cilantro

- Any other toppings of your choice

Directions:

1. Add onion, garlic, and beef to a skillet. Place the skillet over medium heat. Stir on and off. As you stir, break the meat into crumbles.

2. Drain off any fat from the pan and stir in salsa and taco seasoning.

3. Turn down the heat and simmer for about 5 minutes or until thick. Add ⅛ – ¼ cup of water to dilute if necessary.

4. Meanwhile, pierce the sweet potatoes with a fork at several places. Place the sweet potatoes in a microwave-safe bowl and cook on high for 8 to 10 minutes or until fork tender. Turn them after about 4 – 5 minutes of cooking.

5. If they are not cooked through, cook them for a couple of minutes longer.

6. Take them out of the microwave and leave them to cool for a few minutes.

7. Cut into 2 halves lengthwise. Take a fork and loosen the sweet potato pulp.

8. Place 2 sweet potato halves on each serving plate. Divide the taco meat equally between them, add toppings, if using, over the taco meat, and serve.

Taco Bowls

Serves: 2

Nutritional values per serving: 1 bowl

Calories: 380

Fat: 9 g

Carbohydrate: 38 g

Protein: 35 g

Ingredients:

For stir-fry:

- 6 ounces frozen cauliflower rice

- ½ can (from a 15-ounce can) of corn kernels, drained, rinsed

- ½ - 1 jalapeño, sliced

- ½ tablespoon olive oil

- ½ can (from a 15-ounce can) of black beans, drained, rinsed

- 1 medium bell pepper of any color, diced

- Chili powder to taste

For beef taco meat:

- ½ pound lean ground beef

- 2 – 3 cloves garlic, peeled, minced

- ¼ teaspoon kosher salt

- ¼ teaspoon ground cumin

- ¼ cup enchilada sauce or salsa

- ½ medium onion, diced

- 1 teaspoon paprika

- ¼ teaspoon pepper

- Chili powder or chipotle pepper to taste

- ½ can (from 4 ounces can) of diced green chilies

Directions:

1. Place the cauliflower rice in a microwave-safe bowl and cook on high for about 3 to 4 minutes.

2. Meanwhile, pour oil into a nonstick skillet and place it over medium-high heat. You can still make the stir-fry if you do not add the oil. You will also reduce some calories as well as fat.

3. When the oil is hot, add corn, beans, cauliflower rice, and bell pepper and stir. Now do not disturb the vegetables for about 4 to 5 minutes or until slightly charred. Sprinkle chili powder on top.

4. Give it a good stir and cook for about 3 minutes undisturbed or until the underside is slightly charred.

5. Heat another pan over medium heat, add the beef, garlic, and onion, and stir.

6. As you stir, break the beef into crumbles.

7. When the meat is light brown, turn to the heat low.

8. Stir in the spices, chilies, and enchilada sauce. Cook for about 4 to 5 minutes, stirring often. Turn off the heat.

To assemble:

1. Place 1 cup each of corn mixture and taco meat in each bowl.

2. Drizzle lime juice in each bowl.

3. Sprinkle cilantro on top and serve.

Turkey Zucchini Meatloaf with Feta

Serves: 4

Nutritional values per serving: 1 slice

Calories: 254

Fat: 13 g

Carbohydrate: 10 g

Protein: 26 g

Ingredients:

- ¼ cup panko breadcrumbs or breadcrumbs from 1 slice of bread

- 1 pound ground turkey

- 1 teaspoon onion powder

- ½ teaspoon salt

- ½ teaspoon Italian seasoning

- ½ cup crumbled feta cheese

- ½ cup marinara sauce, divided

- 1 teaspoon granulated garlic

- ½ teaspoon pepper

- ½ tablespoon Worcestershire sauce

- 1 cup shredded zucchini, squeezed of excess moisture

- ⅛ cup of nonfat milk or nondairy milk

- 1 egg

Directions:

1. Preheat the oven to 350° F. Coat a baking sheet with some cooking spray.

2. Combine breadcrumbs and milk in a bowl and stir until you have a paste-like consistency.

3. Add turkey, seasonings, feta cheese, and ¼ cup of marinara sauce, egg, Worcestershire sauce, and zucchini into the bowl of breadcrumbs. Mix until well combined but do not over-mix, or the meat will become tough.

4. Transfer the mixture onto the baking sheet and shape it into a loaf.

5. Spoon the remaining marinara sauce on the meatloaf and spread it evenly.

6. Place the baking sheet in the oven and set the timer for about 1 hour or until the internal temperature of the meatloaf shows 160° F on the meat thermometer.

7. Once it is baked, let it rest for 5 minutes on your countertop.

8. Cut into 4 equal slices and serve.

Moroccan Turkey Meatballs

Serves: 8

Nutritional values per serving: 1/8 recipe

Calories: 283

Fat: 10 g

Carbohydrate: 22 g

Protein: 28 g

Ingredients:

For the meatballs:

- 2 pounds of ground turkey
- ½ inch fresh ginger, peeled, finely grated, or minced
- 1 teaspoon ground allspice
- ¼ teaspoon ground cinnamon
- 2 teaspoons ground cumin
- 1 ½ teaspoons ground coriander
- 1 teaspoon garlic powder
- Pepper to taste
- Salt to taste
- ¼ cup chopped parsley
- 1 cup plain breadcrumbs

- 2 large eggs

For the sauce:

- 2 cans (15 ounces each) of tomato sauce

- 1 teaspoon sweet paprika

- Crushed red pepper flakes to taste

- Pepper to taste

- ½ teaspoon ground cumin

- 2 tablespoons tomato paste

- Salt to taste

- Chopped parsley to garnish (optional)

To serve: Optional

- Cauliflower rice

- Brown or white rice

- Couscous

- Whole-wheat spaghetti

- Whole-grain pasta or any pasta of your choice

- Any other grain of your choice

Directions:

1. To make meatballs: Combine ground turkey, egg, ginger, breadcrumbs, parsley, allspice, cumin, coriander, garlic powder, parsley, pepper, and salt in a bowl, making sure not to over-mix.

2. Line a baking sheet with a sheet of parchment paper.

3. Using a medium-sized scoop, scoop out the meat mixture and make small meatballs. Place them on the baking sheet.

4. Place the baking sheet in the refrigerator for 10 minutes.

5. Place a nonstick pan over medium heat. Spray the pan with a little cooking oil spray, heat it and add the meatballs. Cook until brown all over and well-cooked inside.

6. Meanwhile, prepare the sauce: Combine tomato sauce, paprika, red pepper flakes, pepper, cumin, tomato paste, and salt in a saucepan. Place the saucepan over medium heat.

7. Pour the sauce into the skillet with the cooked meatballs and stir, coating them with the sauce. Let the meatballs simmer in the sauce for a few minutes.

8. Garnish with parsley and serve over any of the suggested serving options.

Cannellini Bean and Herbed Ricotta Toast

Serves: 1

Nutritional values per serving: 1

Calories: 132

Fat: 9 g

Carbohydrate: 42 g

Protein: 15 g

Ingredients:

- ¼ cup part-skim ricotta cheese
- 1 slice of sourdough bread
- 1 tablespoon chopped, roasted red bell pepper
- 1 tablespoon chopped mixed fresh herbs
- ½ cup unsalted, cooked, or canned cannellini beans, warmed

Directions:

1. Toast the bread to the desired crispiness.

2. Combine mixed herbs and ricotta in a bowl. Spread the ricotta mixture on one side of the toast.

3. Spread beans over the ricotta. Garnish with roasted red bell pepper pieces and serve.

Black Bean Tostadas with Tofu

Serves: 2

Nutritional values per serving: 1 tostada

Calories: 174

Fat: 6.48 g

Carbohydrate: 20.21 g

Protein: 11.22 g

Ingredients:

- 2 corn tortillas (6 inches each)
- 2 ounces light firm tofu, cubed
- 1 ½ plum tomatoes, cut into ½ inch pieces
- ¾ teaspoon salt-free chili-lime seasoning blend
- ½ cup shredded romaine lettuce
- ⅛ cup nonfat plain Greek yogurt
- 2 lime wedges
- ½ onion, thinly sliced
- 3.5 ounces zucchini, quartered lengthwise, cut into slices crosswise
- ½ cup unsalted cooked or canned black beans, rinsed, drained
- ¼ cup shredded reduced-fat cheddar cheese
- ¼ Hass avocado, peeled, diced

- ¼ cup chopped cilantro

Directions:

1. Preheat the oven to 350° F.

2. Brush oil lightly on either side of the tortillas and lay them on a baking sheet.

3. Place the baking sheet in the oven and bake until they are crispy.

4. Meanwhile, place a nonstick pan over medium-high heat. Spray lightly with cooking spray.

5. Add onion and cook for a couple of minutes. Add the tofu and cook for a few minutes until they turn light brown.

6. Add tomatoes, zucchini, beans, and chili-lime seasoning and stir. Stir often and cook for a few minutes.

7. When the zucchini is tender, turn off the heat.

8. Place the tortillas on individual serving plates. Place half the zucchini mixture on each tortilla.

9. Divide the cheese, lettuce, and cilantro equally among the tortillas.

10. Drizzle a tablespoon of yogurt on each. Garnish with a lime wedge and serve.

Honey Garlic Lime Glazed Shrimp

Serves: 4

Nutritional values per serving: ¼ recipe, without serving options

Calories: 172

Fat: 0.3 g

Carbohydrate: 27 g

Protein: 15 g

Ingredients:

- 2 cups shrimp cooked or raw
- 6 tablespoons honey
- Thinly sliced green onion to garnish
- 4 tablespoons soy sauce
- 6 cloves garlic, peeled, minced
- Juice of 4 limes

Directions:

1. Combine honey, soy sauce, garlic, and lime juice in a pan. Place the pan over low heat and let it heat for about 7 to 8 minutes. Stir on and off.

2. Stir in the shrimp; if they are raw, let them cook for 2 minutes. Flip sides and let them cook for another 2 minutes. If the shrimp are pre-cooked, let them heat for 30 seconds on each side.

3. Garnish with green onions and serve over brown rice or cauliflower rice.

Salmon Foil Packets

Serves: 4

Nutritional values per serving: 1 packet

Calories: 604

Fat: 29 g

Carbohydrate: 31 g

Protein: 56 g

Ingredients:

- 4 salmon filets (about ½ pound each)
- ½ teaspoon freshly ground black pepper or more to taste
- 10 – 12 grape tomatoes, halved
- 12 red baby potatoes, halved
- 1 teaspoon kosher salt, divided
- 2 teaspoons minced garlic
- 8 ounces French beans, trimmed, cut

Directions:

1. Preheat the oven to 400° F.

2. Take 4 large sheets of aluminum foil.

3. Place a salmon filet on the center of each foil. Scatter with potatoes, green beans, garlic, and tomatoes, and season with salt and pepper to taste.

4. Wrap the salmon and vegetables tightly in the foil and place them on a large baking sheet.

5. Put the baking sheet into the oven and cook for 25 minutes or until the internal temperature of the salmon shows 145° F on the meat thermometer.

6. Serve. Be careful when opening the packets; lots of steam can gush out.

Teriyaki Tuna with Pineapple

Serves: 2

Nutritional values per serving: ½ recipe

Calories: 300

Fat: 4.7 g

Carbohydrate: 37.8 g

Protein: 30.7 g

Ingredients:

- 2 tablespoons soy sauce

- ½ tablespoon sugar

- 2 cloves garlic, peeled and chopped

- ½ fresh pineapple, peeled, cored, cut into 4 wedges

- 1 ½ tablespoons dry sherry or fat-free, low-sodium chicken broth

- ½ tablespoon grated fresh ginger

- 2 tuna steaks (5 ounces each)

- ½ red bell pepper, cut into 2 halves

Directions:

1. Add soy sauce, sugar, garlic, ginger, and sherry into a shallow bowl and mix well.

2. Pour half the sauce mixture into another shallow bowl.

3. Add steaks into one of the bowls. Add bell pepper and pineapple to the other bowl.

4. Make sure the tuna, bell pepper, and pineapple are well coated on each side.

5. Keep it covered in the refrigerator for about 15 minutes.

6. Set the oven to broil mode and preheat the oven.

7. Spray a broiler pan with some cooking spray. Remove the tuna, bell pepper, and pineapple from the marinade and place in the broiler pan, and discard the marinade.

8. Place the broiler pan in the oven and broil for 4 – 5 minutes. Baste with the marinade from the bowl of pineapple.

9. Turn the tuna, pineapple, and bell pepper over and broil the other side for 4 – 5 minutes, basting with the marinade.

10. Serve hot.

Cloud Bread Pizza

Serves: 2

Nutritional values per serving: 1 pizza

Calories: 167

Fat: 5 g

Carbohydrate: 7 g

Protein: 18 g

Ingredients:

- 8 large egg whites at room temperature

- 2 teaspoons dried Italian herbs

- 2 tablespoons cornstarch or coconut flour

- ½ teaspoon salt or to taste

For the toppings:

- 4 tablespoons low carb pizza sauce

- 2 tablespoons sliced olives

- 4 tablespoons shredded low-fat cheese

Directions:

1. Preheat the oven to 350° F. Place a sheet of parchment paper on a large baking sheet.

2. Beat egg whites in a bowl until medium peaks are formed (neither too soft nor too stiff).

3. Beat in the cornstarch. Beat until stiff peaks are formed.

4. Divide the whites into 2 portions and place them on the baking sheet, leaving a sufficient gap between them.

5. Spread the whites into a round shape. Bake in the oven until golden brown, about 15 to 17 minutes.

6. Now spread pizza sauce on top of the crusts. Scatter cheese and olives on top and bake for a few minutes until the cheese melts.

7. Cut into wedges and serve.

Mexican Bean Stew

Serves: 8

Nutritional values per serving: ⅛ recipe

Calories: 274

Fat: 5 g

Carbohydrate: 67 g

Protein: 15 g

Ingredients:

- ½ tablespoon vegetable oil

- 1 red onion, finely chopped

- 2 teaspoons ground cumin

- 2 teaspoons dried oregano

- 2 cans (15 ounces each) of black beans, rinsed, drained

- 2 cans (8 ounces each) of corn kernels, drained

- 2 cups vegetable broth

- 2 teaspoons sugar

- 4 cups cooked brown rice

- 8 cloves garlic, peeled, finely minced

- 2 jalapeños, deseeded, finely minced

- 2 teaspoons paprika

- ½ teaspoon black pepper

- 2 cans (15 ounces each) of chickpeas, rinsed, drained

- 2 cans (14 ounces each) of crushed tomatoes

- 2 teaspoons salt

Directions:

1. Pour oil into a pot and place it over medium heat. When the oil is hot, add onion, garlic, and jalapeño and stir. Cook until light brown.

2. Stir in the seasonings. Keep stirring for a few seconds until you get a nice aroma, taking care not to burn the spices.

3. Stir in chickpeas, black beans, tomatoes, corn, sugar, salt, and stork.

4. Turn down the heat to medium-low and simmer until the stew is thickened to the desired consistency.

5. Garnish with cilantro and serve with brown rice.

Hummus and Veggie Wrap-Up

Serves: 2

Nutritional values per serving: 1 wrap

Calories: 235

Fat: 8 g

Carbohydrate: 32 g

Protein: 7 g

Ingredients:

- 4 tablespoons hummus
- ½ cup torn mixed salad greens
- ¼ cup thinly sliced cucumber
- ¼ cup shredded carrot
- 2 whole-wheat tortillas (8 inches each)
- ¼ cup finely chopped onion
- ¼ cup alfalfa sprouts
- 2 tablespoons balsamic vinaigrette

Directions:

1. Spread 2 tablespoons of hummus on each tortilla.

2. Scatter ¼ cup of salad greens over each, followed by half the onion and cucumber.

3. Divide the alfalfa sprouts and carrots equally among the tortillas.

4. Drizzle a tablespoon of vinaigrette over each tortilla. Wrap tightly and fasten with toothpicks to serve.

Chapter 8:

Dishes for Special Occasions

Squash and Chicken Stew

Serves: 2 – 3

Nutritional values per serving: 1-½ cups without couscous

Calories: 384

Fat: 14 g

Carbohydrate: 31 g

Protein: 37 g

Ingredients:

- 1 pound boneless, skinless chicken thighs, chopped into ½ inch chunks

- 1 ½ cups peeled, deseeded, cubed butternut squash

- ½ small onion, sliced; separate the layers

- ½ teaspoon salt

- ¼ teaspoon coriander

- ½ teaspoon ground cumin

- ¼ teaspoon ground pepper

- 1 tablespoon minced fresh parsley

- ½ can (from 28 ounces can) of stewed tomatoes, chopped

- 1 medium green bell pepper, cut into ½ inch pieces

- ½ cup water

- Hot cooked couscous to serve (optional)

Directions:

1. Combine chicken, vegetables, spices, tomatoes, and water in a pot.

2. Place the pot over medium heat. When the mixture starts boiling, turn down the heat and cook until the chicken is cooked through.

3. Serve chicken and vegetables over couscous if desired.

Beef and Mushrooms

Serves: 2

Nutritional values per serving: ⅛ recipe, without serving options

Calories: 410.5

Fat: 23.9 g

Carbohydrate: 12.4 g

Protein: 23.9 g

Ingredients:

- ½ pound lean beef stew meat

- ¼ cup water or more if required

- 4 ounces fresh mushrooms, sliced or halved

- ½ can low-fat cream of mushroom soup

- ½ packet dry onion soup mix

To serve:

- Whole-grain noodles or pasta

- Gluten-free pasta or noodles

- Brown rice

- Cauliflower rice

- Whole grain bread

Directions:

1. Place a pot over medium-high heat. Add beef and cook until brown.

2. Stir in the mushrooms.

3. Whisk together water, mushroom soup, and soup mix in a bowl and add to the pot.

4. Stir well. Cover and cook until the meat is tender, stirring on and off. Add some water if the meat is uncooked and there is no liquid in the pot.

5. Serve hot with any of the suggested serving options.

Seafood Stew

Serves: 3

Nutritional values per serving: 1/3 recipe, without bread

Calories: 184

Fat: 2 g

Carbohydrate: 18 g

Protein: 26 g

Ingredients:

- 1 pound seafood, thawed if frozen
- ½ can (from 28 ounces can) of crushed tomatoes
- 1 ½ cups vegetable broth
- ½ pound yellow potatoes, cut into bite-size pieces
- ½ tablespoon tomato paste
- 2 cloves garlic, peeled, minced
- ¼ cup chopped onion
- ½ teaspoon dried basil
- ¼ teaspoon celery salt
- A pinch of cayenne pepper
- ½ teaspoon dried thyme
- ½ teaspoon dried oregano

- Pepper to taste

- ⅛ teaspoon crushed red pepper flakes

- Salt to taste

- Chopped parsley to garnish

- Crusty bread to serve (optional)

Directions:

1. Combine tomatoes, broth, potatoes, tomato paste, garlic, onion, herbs, celery salt, and spices in a pot.

2. Place the pot over high heat. When the mixture starts boiling, turn down the heat to low. Cook covered until the potatoes are fork tender.

3. Stir in the seafood and cook until the seafood is well cooked.

4. Garnish with parsley and serve with crusty bread if using.

Black Bean Chili

Serves: 2 – 3

Nutritional values per serving: 1-½ cups, without toppings

Calories: 273

Fat: 1.6 g

Carbohydrate: 59.2 g

Protein: 17.5 g

Ingredients:

- 1 can (10 ounces) tomatoes with green chilies, with its liquid
- 1 can (15 ounces) of black beans, rinsed, drained
- 1 tablespoon chili powder or to taste

Directions:

1. Take about ½ cup of black beans and mash them up with a fork until coarse in texture.

2. Transfer into a saucepan. Add the rest of the beans, chili powder, and tomatoes and stir.

3. Place the saucepan over medium heat. When it starts boiling, turn the heat low and cook for about 12 – 15 minutes. Dilute with some water; if necessary, stir on and off.

4. Serve with toppings of your choice.

Lentil and Rice Loaf

Serves: 20

Nutritional values per serving: 1 slice

Calories: 163

Fat: 5.2 g

Carbohydrate: 26.2 g

Protein: 6 g

Ingredients:

- 3 ½ cups water

- 1 cup uncooked short-grain brown rice, rinsed

- 1 cup uncooked brown or green lentils, rinsed

- 4 teaspoons poultry seasoning

- 2 medium onions, chopped

- 1 cup sliced celery ribs

- 1 ½ cups old-fashioned rolled oats

- 1 cup chopped walnuts or pecans (optional)

- 4 teaspoons minced fresh thyme or 2 teaspoons dried thyme

- 10 medium white or cremini mushrooms, chopped

- 2 tablespoons finely chopped garlic

- 2 cans (6 ounces each) of tomato paste

- 2 tablespoons minced fresh sage or 1 tablespoon dried rubbed sage

- 1 tablespoon minced fresh rosemary or 1 ½ teaspoons dried rosemary

- 2 teaspoons granulated onions

Directions:

1. If you have the time, soak the rice and lentils in water for about 2 hours.

2. Combine lentils, rice, water, granulated onion, and poultry seasoning in a saucepan.

3. Place the saucepan over high heat and bring it to a boil.

4. Turn down the heat to low and cook covered for about 45 minutes or until tender and there is no water left in the pot.

5. Turn off the heat and do not uncover for 10 minutes.

6. Meanwhile, place a pan over high heat and add a couple of tablespoons of water.

7. When the water starts boiling, stir in the mushrooms, onion, and celery. Stir on and off and cook for about 4 – 5 minutes. Add a little more water if required.

8. Stir in the garlic and dried herbs and cook until the vegetables are tender. Turn off the heat.

9. Preheat the oven to 350° F. Take 2 loaf pans of 9 x 5 x 3 inches each and line them with parchment paper.

10. Add mushroom mixture, lentil mixture, oats, walnuts, tomato paste, and fresh herbs, if using, into a bowl and stir until well combined.

11. Place the mixture in batches in the food processor bowl. Give short pulses until well incorporated and slightly chunky as well.

12. Divide the mixture equally in the loaf pan, pressing it onto the bottom of the pan.

13. Cover the pans with aluminum foil. Place them in the oven and set the timer for 40 minutes.

14. Uncover and continue baking until brown on top.

15. Take out the loaf pans from the oven and let them cool for 10 minutes.

16. Cut each loaf into 10 equal slices and serve.

17. You can store leftovers in an airtight container in the refrigerator. Warm the slices in a microwave and serve.

Smoky Lentil and Quinoa Soup

Serves: 8

Nutritional values per serving: ⅛ serving

Calories: 305

Fat: 2.6 g

Carbohydrate: 56.5 g

Protein: 16.8 g

Ingredients:

- ½ cup water

- 4 ribs celery, diced

- 4 cloves garlic, peeled, minced

- 4 large carrots, diced

- 2 small onions, diced

- 2 teaspoons smoked paprika

- 2 teaspoons dried thyme

- ¼ teaspoon ground or grated nutmeg

- 2 teaspoons ground cumin

- 2 teaspoons dried basil

- 2 cups dried lentils (French or green or brown), rinsed, soaked in water for a couple of hours

- 1 cup dried quinoa, rinsed

- 4 – 6 bay leaves

- 2 – 4 tablespoons of balsamic vinegar

- 2 cans (15 ounces each) of diced tomatoes or 4 large fresh tomatoes, diced

- 12 – 14 cups vegetable broth or water, or use a mixture of both

- Chopped parsley to garnish

- Salt to taste

- Pepper to taste

Directions:

1. Add ¼ cup of water into a large pot or Dutch oven and let it heat over medium heat.

2. When the water is hot, add the vegetables and cook for about 5 minutes. Add more water if needed to stop the vegetables from burning.

3. Stir in the spices and cook for a couple of minutes until you get a nice aroma.

4. Stir in the quinoa, lentils, bay leaves, tomatoes, broth, salt, and pepper. When the mixture starts boiling, reduce the heat and cook covered until the lentils and quinoa are tender. Stir every 5 – 7 minutes.

5. Turn off the heat, stir the balsamic vinegar in, and discard the bay leaves.

6. Garnish with parsley and serve.

Cheeseburger Casserole

Serves: 4

Nutritional values per serving: ¼ recipe

Calories: 194

Fat: 10 g

Carbohydrate: 5 g

Protein: 21 g

Ingredients:

- 4 ounces low-carb macaroni, like Low-carb bread company macaroni

- 1 small onion, chopped

- ½ pound lean ground beef

- ½ tablespoon Worcestershire sauce

- ¼ cup finely grated parmesan cheese

- ½ tablespoon olive oil

- 3 slices bacon, chopped

- 8 ounces tomato sauce passata

- ¾ cup grated mozzarella cheese

Directions:

1. Preheat the oven to 350° F. Coat a small baking dish (about 5 – 6 inches) with a little cooking spray.

2. Cook the macaroni as per the directions given on the package.

3. Pour oil into a nonstick pan and place it over medium heat. Add onion and cook for a couple of minutes.

4. Stir in the bacon and cook for a minute before adding the beef. Stir to crumble the meat into smaller pieces and cook until it is no longer pink.

5. Stir in the tomato sauce. Add the drained pasta and mix well, then add half the Parmesan and mozzarella.

6. Give the mixture a good stir and turn off the heat. Spread the mixture into the baking dish.

7. Sprinkle remaining mozzarella and Parmesan on top. Place the baking dish in the oven and cook for 10 to 15 minutes or until the cheese melts and starts to brown.

Quinoa Spanish Rice

Serves: 3

Nutritional values per serving: 1/3 recipe

Calories: 130

Fat: 1.9 g

Carbohydrate: 24.2 g

Protein: 4.9 g

Ingredients:

- ½ tablespoon olive oil or 2 tablespoons water
- ½ green bell pepper, finely diced
- ½ cup quinoa, rinsed, drained
- 1 cup low-sodium vegetable broth
- ¼ teaspoon garlic powder
- ¼ teaspoon onion powder (optional)
- Chopped cilantro to garnish
- ½ cup finely diced onion
- 1 large clove garlic, minced or ½ teaspoon extra garlic powder
- ½ tablespoon tomato paste
- ½ cup diced tomatoes
- ¼ teaspoon dried oregano

- Salt to taste

- Pepper to taste

Directions:

1. Add oil or water into a skillet and place it over medium-high heat.

2. When hot, add onion and bell pepper and cook for a couple of minutes.

3. Stir in the quinoa and garlic. Stir on and off until the quinoa is light brown and toasted.

4. Stir in the tomato paste, tomatoes, broth, oregano, pepper, garlic powder, onion powder, and salt.

5. When the mixture starts boiling, turn the heat to low and cook covered until almost no liquid is left in the pan.

6. Turn off the heat, uncover the pan, and fluff the quinoa grains using a fork. Cover the pot and let it rest for 15 minutes.

7. Serve.

Chicken Marrakesh

Serves: 4

Nutritional values per serving: ¼ recipe without serving options

Calories: 290

Fat: 2 g

Carbohydrate: 36 g

Protein: 31 g

Ingredients:

- ½ onion, sliced

- 1 pound skinless, boneless chicken breast halves, cut into 2-inch chunks

- 1 large sweet potato, peeled, diced

- 1 clove garlic, peeled, minced

- 1 large carrot, peeled, diced

- ½ can (from a 15-ounce can) of chickpeas, drained, rinsed

- ½ can (from 14.5 ounces can) of diced tomatoes

- ¼ teaspoon ground cumin

- 1/8 teaspoon ground cinnamon

- ½ teaspoon dried parsley

- ¼ teaspoon turmeric powder

- ¼ teaspoon ground black pepper

- ½ teaspoon salt

Directions:

1. Add garlic, onion, sweet potato, carrot, chicken, and chickpeas into a heavy pot or Dutch oven.

2. Combine cumin, pepper, salt, parsley, turmeric, and cinnamon in a bowl.

3. Sprinkle the spice mixture over the ingredients in the pot and mix well.

4. Stir in tomatoes and place the pot over medium heat. When the mixture starts boiling, turn the heat low and cook covered until the vegetables are tender and the sauce is thick. Stir occasionally.

5. Serve over couscous or any other grain of your choice.

Pepper, Date, and Harissa Tagine

Serves: 12

Nutritional values per serving: 1/12 recipe tagine and salad without serving options

Calories: 225

Fat: 2.3 g

Carbohydrate: 40 g

Protein: 6.9 g

Ingredients:

- 4 onions, diced

- 8 cloves garlic, peeled, sliced

- 1 teaspoon turmeric powder

- Juice of 2 lemons

- Zest of 2 lemons, grated

- 4 tablespoons honey

- 2 teaspoons ground cinnamon

- 2 tablespoons ground coriander

- Freshly ground pepper to taste

- 3 red bell peppers, deseeded, cut into 1-inch squares

- 3 yellow bell peppers, deseeded, cut into 1-inch squares

- 3 orange bell peppers, deseeded, cut into 1-inch squares

- 4 sticks of celery, cut into thin slices

- 2 vegetable stock cubes, crumbled

- 4 cans (14 ounces) of chopped tomatoes with their juices

- 4 tablespoons rose harissa or harissa

- 12 ounces dates, pitted, quartered

- Salt to taste

- 4 cups hot water

- Fresh herbs of your choice to garnish

- Hummus to serve

For the crunchy salad:

- 2 cucumbers or fennel bulbs, sliced

- 4 teaspoons fresh lemon juice or to taste

- 10.5 ounces plain nonfat yogurt

- A large handful of fresh mint leaves, chopped

Directions:

1. Add onions, garlic, celery, turmeric powder, and stock cubes into a heavy pot or Dutch oven. Add about 4 cups of hot water and stir well.

2. Strain the cans of tomatoes into a strainer over a bowl and collect the juice. Set aside the tomatoes.

3. Pour the tomato juice into the pot and stir it well.

4. Cover the pot and let it cook for about 45 minutes.

5. Add the lemon juice, strained tomatoes, harissa, cinnamon, coriander, salt, honey, and pepper, and mix well.

6. Stir in the dates and bell peppers and give it a good stir. Cover the pot once again and turn down the heat to low. Cook for about an hour until the sauce is thick and the flavors blend.

7. To make the crunchy salad: Combine cucumber, lemon juice, yogurt, and mint leaves in a bowl.

8. Serve tagine in bowls. Garnish with fresh herbs.

9. Serve with flatbreads or couscous along with hummus.

Chapter 9:

Things That You Need to Understand about the Noom Dieting Lifestyle

Tasks to Follow

There are certain things that you should follow while doing the Noom diet. These tasks are crucial to follow and help you produce the best results while doing the Noom diet lifestyle.

Log Meals

The first thing you must do regularly while following the Noom diet is to update your meals. By logging your meals regularly, you can check how many calories you have consumed and what kind of food you should eat more or less of. It can also help you understand the intricacies of the color categories of the Noom diet and help you keep an eye on your weight.

Access Workout Plans

The Noom app allows you access to various workout plans according to the requirements of your body. You can also edit the workout plans according to your needs and change them to suit your routine and schedule. You can either add or subtract activities from the overall fitness plan.

Track Exercise

Along with meals, it is crucial to track your exercise regularly on the

Noom app. This way, you can check how many calories you regularly burn and whether you are on track. It can also help you check whether you should increase the amount, time, and intensity of any exercise or reduce it.

Rate Your Motivation Level

By rating your motivation level from time to time, your coach can understand whether they should send you more motivating stuff. It can also point out where you are lagging and need more help. Remember, Noom is all about support, and you are not using it properly if you are not asking for support from the app.

Read Articles

What separates Noom from any other fitness or diet program is that it does not just work on food and exercise, but it also works on your psychology. It tries to change your mindset so that you can experience sustained weight loss that can be maintained without any hassle. For this, it is necessary to read the articles that are sent on the app from time to time. Try to read at least five minutes of the article every day. You can increase the time according to your wish and requirements.

Search Recipes

Noom app recommends various food items across its color-coded categories. You can look for recipes incorporating ingredients from all three categories or search for recipes you can change according to your tastes. This book contains amazing recipes that can help you get started.

Set Goals

Without goals, you are just like a decapitated chicken. You may have a lot of energy, but if you don't know how, where, and when to spend it, then it is useless. Noom is an amazing resource for losing weight; however, the app will not provide appropriate results without properly defined goals. Fix some goals and try to chase them.

Receive Support from a Personal Health Coach

The Noom app provides a personal health coach with whom you can talk twice a week. Noom trains these health coaches, who are certified dieticians or gym trainers. Talk to them repeatedly to stay motivated and receive crucial support.

What Can You Eat on the Noom Diet Plan?

The thing that separates Noom from other fitness or diet plans is that it is supposed to be sustainable. Unlike fad diets that are supposed to show instant results, the Noom diet takes time. But the results of the Noom diet are long-lasting and sustainable; they don't disappear randomly. The results are not short-lived and do not negatively affect your body. The goal of Noom is to find a new normal, a new lifestyle that you can follow without any issues for a long time. You should not feel disappointed, angry, or cranky while losing weight, as this form of weight loss is not sustainable. By changing your mindset and lifestyle, the Noom diet helps you lose weight in a much more long-lasting way.

Benefits of the Noom Diet App

It Focuses on Calorie Density and Nutrients

It is crucial to consume proper amounts of nutrients and calories. The Noom diet allows you to consume high amounts of nutrients without putting a lot of empty calories in your body. Foods containing low calories are considered to be better for the body as they often have high nutrients and reduce hunger. These food items can help you lose weight and can also reduce the risk of chronic diseases and disorders such as cardiac arrest.

Inclusivity of Food

What separates Noom from any other fitness app or diet plan is that it allows you to eat anything you want. In other diets, many food items are restricted, and you are forced to eat only 'clean' foods. The Noom diet is much more flexible and allows you to consume whatever you want. The app also has an extensive library of recipes where you can find recipes that suit your taste buds. You can also customize the recipes according to your requirements.

Behavioral Change

Noom helps you lose weight by helping you adopt a healthier lifestyle by changing your mindset. It helps you develop new healthy habits, so you don't fall off the track and start gaining weight again. If your habits do not change, you are bound to regain any lost weight. Noom helps you by providing all the necessary tools and information to change your mindset and help you lose weight.

Noom Diet Reviews

There are numerous reviews available about the Noom diet online. Most of these reviews praise the following factors that make Noom the best diet app.

- It is a weight loss program based on a psychological approach, making it much more sustainable and easier to follow.

- It is a responsible program that provides ample support and motivation from time to time.

- Instead of focusing on short-term and temporary weight loss, this program focuses on long-term and sustainable weight loss, making it quite popular.

- Unlike other weight loss programs, it does not restrict any foods. It allows you to eat whatever you want, albeit in different proportions.

- It promotes behavioral changes making it much more sustainable.

- The color-coded system of the diet has been praised by many for being easy to understand and follow. It allows people to consume healthy food items without consuming many calories.

- The goals can be adjusted according to the requirements and likings of the users.

Another factor that is celebrated quite often about Noom is that it has trained and practical coaches who support and motivate the users from time to time.

Chapter 10:

Noom Diet – Here's Why

The Noom diet has many benefits that make it best for sustained weight loss. This chapter contains some of these benefits and reasons for starting the Noom diet immediately.

Inflammation

Inflammation is a common factor in every human being as it is a part of our body's defense mechanism. In this, the immune system understands that there is something foreign and harmful in the body and tries to heal it. Inflammation can be chronic or acute. While there are two kinds of inflammation, the Noom diet can help you in both to a certain extent.

Acute Inflammation

Microbial invasion, trauma, or noxious compounds generally cause acute inflammation. As the name suggests, this form of inflammation starts quickly and can become potent in an extremely short time. The symptoms, such as acute pneumonia and cellulitis, may last for a few days. Subacute inflammation lies in the middle of chronic and acute inflammation and may last for 2-6 weeks. While this inflammation is sudden, the Noom diet can help you reduce the chances of it occurring. Acute inflammation is often caused due to obesity, a common factor that can be reduced with the help of the Noom diet.

Chronic Inflammation

Chronic inflammation is also known as long-term or slow inflammation. This form of inflammation can last anywhere between several months to years. The effects and extent of chronic inflammation differ from person to person and vary according to the cause of the injury. The effects are also based on the ability of the body to recover and overcome the damage. The Noom diet can help you reduce this inflammation in stages. Here are some of the risk factors of chronic inflammation and a brief look at how they can be targeted with the help of the Noom diet.

Risk Factors

Many risk factors are responsible for low-level inflammatory response.

Obesity

The fat tissue secretes a variety of inflammatory mediators and multiple adipokines, which can lead to inflammation. The body mass index of a person is directly proportional to the number of cytokines secreted. Metabolic syndrome is a great example of this. As the Noom diet is highly effective in reducing weight and tackling the symptoms as well as causes of obesity, it can largely help you to reduce the onset of inflammation.

Age

As a person ages, the number of several inflammatory molecules increases as well. Mitochondrial dysfunction and the accumulation of free radicals is a prime cause of inflammation due to age. Various other age-related factors are also responsible for increasing inflammation with time. While the Noom diet cannot reverse or stop aging, it can reduce the accumulation of free radicals, a common cause of aging.

Diet

A diet that is rich in trans-fat, saturated fats, processed foods, and refined sugar can lead to the production of pro-inflammatory molecules. This is especially prominent in people who are overweight or have diabetes. The Noom diet, with its focus on healthy and non-processed foods, can effectively tackle inflammation caused by diet. The Noom diet can also help you curate a highly efficient diet that reduces the effects of present chronic inflammation.

Low Sex Hormones

Sex hormones such as estrogen and testosterone can reduce the secretion and production of many inflammatory markers. Reduced amounts of sex hormones can lead to several inflammatory diseases.

Smoking

Cigarette smoking can reduce the production of anti-inflammatory molecules, which may lead to inflammation. While the Noom diet does not tackle smoking directly, the psychological tactics learned through the app, such as CBT, can be applied to smoking and other harmful habits.

Sleep Disorders and Stress

Emotional as well as physical stress can lead to the release of cytokine. Stress can also lead to the development of sleep disorders. People with irregular sleep schedules are more likely to develop chronic inflammation than people with a proper sleep schedule. Sleep is also affected by one's weight and health. It has been noted that being overweight can be quite bad for one's quality as well as the duration of sleep. Obesity can also lead to sleep apnea and other similar problems. As the Noom diet targets obesity, it can help you sleep better.

Symptoms of Chronic Inflammation

Some of the prominent and common symptoms of chronic inflammation are as follows:

- Chronic insomnia and fatigue

- Arthralgia

- Myalgia

- Body pain

- Anxiety

- Depression

- Mood disorders

- Diarrhea

- Constipation

- Acid reflux

- Weight gain

- Frequent infections

Complications

While chronic inflammation progresses quite slowly compared to acute inflammation, it is still considered a big threat to the health and longevity of people and can lead to the development of many different chronic diseases and disorders. Inflammation is considered to be a major contributor to a variety of diseases and disorders. Some of these diseases and disorders include:

Cardiovascular Diseases

It has been observed that there is a relationship between cardiovascular diseases and inflammation. Atherosclerosis can lead to low-grade inflammation, increasing the risk of cardiovascular problems such as stroke, myocardial infarction, etc.

Cancer

Chronic low-level inflammation can also lead to the development of a variety of cancers, such as prostate, kidney, hepatocellular, ovarian, colorectal, pancreatic, lung, and mesothelioma.

Diabetes

Macrophage is an immune cell that can enter pancreatic tissues leading to the development of diabetes. Cellular and circulating biomarkers both say that diabetes is a chronic inflammatory disease. Macrovascular as well as microvascular problems are associated with diabetes and are chronic. Diabetes can increase the risk of various microvascular complications such as neuropathy, diabetic retinopathy, nephropathy, etc. It can also increase the risk of macrovascular complications such as heart attacks and strokes. According to the studies mentioned earlier in this book, the Noom diet can prove to be quite useful in tackling diabetes.

Allergic Asthma

Allergic asthma is another issue that can be caused due to chronic inflammation. It can lead to inappropriate immune response and may even lead to inflammation in the airways, which can induce tissue remodeling and reduce airway function as well.

Rheumatoid Arthritis

The case of chronic inflammation, which is generally the result of various environmental factors such as infections and smoking, can lead to a systematic autoimmune response that can lead to local inflammation in joints. It can also lead to inflammation of the immune cells and may lead to the release of cytokines. Chronic inflammation in the synovium may also worsen the radiographic progression and prognosis of the disease.

Obesity, too, can cause joint pains and many other problems. The Noom diet can help you reduce weight and thus the chances of developing arthritis.

COPD

COPD, or Chronic obstructive pulmonary disease, is an obstructive lung disease generally resulting from chronic inflammation. This sort of inflammation is seen in the case of irritants and can lead to long-term breathing problems.

Chronic Kidney Disease

Chronic Kidney disease, also known as CKD, is generally a result of low-grade inflammation. This disease is often symptomatic and can lead to the retention of many inflammatory molecules in the blood, increasing the mortality rate. It can also lead to the development of amyloidosis, leading to extreme and serious renal complications.

As the Noom diet tries to focus on clean eating, it can help you consume foods that are not harmful to the body and can also serve to detox your body, thus helping the function of the kidneys.

Alzheimer's Disease

Chronic inflammation of a low grade can lead to dementia and cognitive decline in the case of older adults.

IBD

IBD, or Inflammatory Bowel Disease, is considered to be a group of chronic inflammatory disorders that affect the digestive tract. It can start as ulcerative colitis and lead to long-lasting ulcers and inflammations of the large intestine. It can also lead to Crohn's disease and can cause inflammation of the digestive tract and the rectum. It can also spread to other digestive system tissues, including the esophagus, mouth, anus, and stomach.

The focus on clean eating that is present in the Noom diet can help you tackle a lot of digestive problems, which in turn can keep the digestive as well as the excretory system healthy.

Treatment/Management

Dietary and lifestyle changes are often recommended to reduce or remove inflammation triggers. These changes can also reduce chronic inflammation. Weight loss has the most efficient and potent result on chronic inflammation. Patients with psoriatic arthritis, which is another name for chronic inflammatory arthritis, have shown quite a significant improvement in their disorder after losing weight. Here are a few ways to manage chronic inflammation:

Low-glycemic diet: A diet with a high glycemic index can lead to various problems, such as coronary heart disease, stroke, and type-2 diabetes mellitus. It is therefore recommended to reduce the number of foods that lead to inflammation in your diet. These foods include fructose corn syrup, processed foods, sodas, refined sugars, refined carbohydrates, etc. Followers of the Noom diet generally follow a low-glycemic diet.

Reduce intake of total saturated fat and trans fats: Omega 3 polyunsaturated fats are supposed to be anti-inflammatory; however, various synthetic trans fats and dietary saturated fats can lead to inflammation. Packaged and processed foods generally contain a lot of trans fats. These food items include vegetable oils, processed seed oils, baked goods, corn oil, soybean oil, etc. It is recommended to reduce these items from your diet as they can be quite harmful to your health.

- **Fruits and vegetables:** Various fruits and vegetables contain high amounts of polyphenols, natural antioxidants, and various anti-inflammatory compounds that can help you defeat inflammation. These vegetables and fruits include cabbage, blueberries, brussels sprouts, apples, cauliflower, broccoli, etc. Cherry, as well as cherry juice, can reduce IL-1 and is supposed to be uricosuric, which can help in inflammation related to gout

- **Fiber:** Consuming high amounts of insoluble and dietary soluble fiber can reduce the levels of TNF-alpha and IL-6. High intake of dietary soluble and insoluble fiber is associated with lowering levels of IL-6 and TNF-alpha.

- **Nuts:** Nuts such as almonds can reduce the risk of inflammation and cardiovascular diseases.

- **Green and black tea polyphenols**: Tea polyphenols can significantly bring down the CRP levels.

- **Curcumin**: This is one of the main components of turmeric. It can reduce various inflammations and inflammatory diseases quite efficiently.

- **Fish Oil:** Fish oil is an excellent source of omega-3 fatty acids. The more amount of omega-3 you consume, the lower the levels of CRP, TNF-alpha, and IL-6 will be.

- **Mung bean:** Mung bean is a legume that contains high amounts of isovitexin, vitexin, and other flavonoids. It is a traditional food, especially in the Indian subcontinent, and is often used as a herbal medicine there. It is supposed to have a lot of anti-inflammatory effects.

- **Micronutrients:** Micronutrients such as Vitamin E, Vitamin D, Magnesium, selenium, and zinc can reduce inflammation. Magnesium is one of the most potent anti-inflammatory micronutrients, and it can reduce the activity of IL-6, hs-CRP, and TNF-alpha. Vitamin D reduces and suppresses inflammatory mediators and thus reduces inflammation. It reduces mediators such as nuclear factor kappa-light-chain-enhancer of B cells and prostaglandins. Zinc, vitamin E, and selenium serve as antioxidants in the body.

- **Sesame Lignans:** Consuming sesame oil regularly can reduce the synthesis of various hypotensive chemicals such as thromboxanes, leukotrienes, and prostaglandin.

Thus, the Noom diet is one of the best options to tackle chronic inflammation as it incorporates most of the suggested diet changes recommended to avoid problems associated with chronic inflammation. Food items such as whole grains, fruits, vegetables, etc., form an integral part of the Noom diet, while items high in harmful fats should be avoided while following this diet.

Physical Exercise

Exercise, too, can reduce the number of cytokines and pro-inflammatory molecules. Exercise, paired with diet, can surely help you defeat inflammation.

The Noom diet can help you overcome inflammation and make you feel healthy and active. It can reduce the chance of getting other health issues associated with inflammation.

Heart Disorders

Many different heart conditions and problems that occur due to various reasons are collectively known as heart disease.

It is necessary to discuss your heart problems or conditions with a certified health professional. It would be even better if you could discuss it with a heart specialist. These professionals can help you with the correct diagnosis and the name of your problem. They can also help you devise a plan to treat the disorder or disease. Generally, losing weight and having a healthy diet are key factors in reducing heart disease risks. This makes the Noom diet an ideal way to avoid complications associated with heart disease.

Heart disease and disorders can affect the way your heart can function. They reduce efficiency and ultimately can damage the heart irrevocably. It can be quite traumatic and troublesome to be diagnosed with a heart condition; however, a lot of support and information may help you understand your condition and overcome it. Understanding what you have and what can be done about it can reduce the worry associated with the disorder. Some common heart diseases affect a large chunk of the population worldwide. As it is clear that most of these diseases result from obesity, it makes sense that the Noom diet can help you tackle most of them quite efficiently.

Coronary Heart Disease

This is the most common heart condition all over the world. This happens when the coronary arteries, i.e., the heart's blood vessels, get blocked or narrow, which may lead to an inadequate supply of blood to the heart. In severe cases, it may lead to a heart attack, angina, or both. As an excess of fat generally blocks blood vessels, losing weight with the help of the Noom diet can help you reduce the risk of coronary heart disease.

Angina

Angina is the discomfort or pain in your jaw, arm, chest, stomach, or neck. This occurs when the blood supply to your heart becomes restricted due to the blocking or narrowing of your arteries. This form of clogging is also known as atheroma. Angina is not considered an illness; rather, it is a prominent symptom of coronary heart disease.

Angina is your heart telling you that it is not getting adequate oxygen, especially when you are stressed or doing something strenuous. Many people can guess how much activity is necessary to trigger an angina attack. Such forms of angina are known as stable angina.

Suppose you tend to experience unexplained chest pain from time to time. In that case, it is required to seek urgent medical advice immediately. You will have to undergo an overall health assessment to diagnose the root cause of your pain. In some cases, the cause might be acute and not risky; in other cases, it might be a sign of something more severe.

Ideally, it is recommended to reduce the risk of angina before its onset by reducing weight and eating healthily as it is prescribed in the Noom diet.

Unstable Angina

Another form of angina is known as unstable angina. An undiagnosed pain in the chest or the sudden worsening of already present angina is known as unstable angina. This generally happens when the blood flow to the heart is restricted suddenly and severely. In this case, the propensity and severity of angina attack increase and enhance. The attacks become more frequent with less and less activity.

These attacks may happen anytime, including during sleep which may jolt and wake you up. These attacks can last up to 10 minutes. If you experience these attacks, you must consult a doctor immediately as you may have to be hospitalized for the same.

Until the tests are done to confirm the diagnosis of the disorder, this condition is sometimes known as ACS or Acute Coronary Syndrome.

Heart Attack

This is another common condition that happens all around the world. It is also known as MI or myocardial infarction. This condition happens when the blood supply to any part or parts of your heart muscles gets blocked completely. This generally happens due to a piece of fatty material breaking off and clogging any coronary artery, thus creating a blood clot. This can damage your heart muscle in part connected to the coronary artery.

This is another disorder that happens due to the blockage of arteries. As said earlier, the Noom diet can help you reduce the number and severity of blockages by helping you cut down on harmful fats and also helping you reduce your weight.

Heart Failure

Suppose the pumping action of the heart cannot work efficiently. In that case, the heart muscles cannot meet your body's demands for oxygen and blood. This leads to various symptoms, including shortness of breath, fatigue, etc. This condition is known as heart failure as the heart ceases to function efficiently in this condition.

Arrhythmia (Abnormal Heart Rhythms)

The heart muscles have an electrical system responsible for creating and stimulating the heartbeat. If this system gets disturbed or interrupted, the heart can beat irregularly, either too slow (bradycardia), fast (tachycardia), or both. This condition is known as arrhythmia.

Valve Disease

The valves of the heart close and open to control the flow of blood through the heart. If the workload of your heart increases exponentially, the valves may become strained and may lead to various symptoms, including:

- Swollen ankles
- Shortness of breath
- Fatigue
- Dizziness
- Angina
- Palpitation
- Fainting

High Blood Pressure

Another common condition that generally affects the heart is hypertension or high blood pressure. While this condition is not a disease, it may be a gateway to other serious diseases and disorders. such as heart attacks, coronary heart disease, and strokes.

Eating junk food and food with little to no nutrients in large quantities (i.e., red foods) is a significant cause of hypertension. Following the Noom diet can help you reduce the risk of high blood pressure.

Congenital Heart Conditions

Congenital heart conditions generally occur when a defect or abnormality is present in the heart's structure while the fetus is developing in the mother's womb. Babies can be born with either one or a combination of many defects. Many congenital heart defects are life-threatening and may prove fatal right after birth or over some time.

Inherited Heart Conditions

Inherited conditions are passed on through families. They are often known as genetic heart conditions or familial heart conditions.

They can be life-threatening and can affect people of all age groups. They can often be asymptomatic and are often diagnosed when the patient passes away suddenly. These conditions are different from congenital heart conditions. However, some congenital heart conditions can also be inherited.

Congenital and inherited heart conditions are uncontrollable and cannot be cured without constant medical intervention. However, inherited heart conditions can be prevented in children if the family stays healthy with the help of diets and exercise routines such as the Noom diet.

Diabetes

According to research studies mentioned earlier, the Noom diet can help people who are prediabetic to reduce the risk of getting diabetes. For people who already have diabetes, the Noom diet can reduce risks associated with the disorder and can help you maintain a much healthier lifestyle. This is true in Type 2 diabetes, and research is still underway for type 1 diabetes.

Other Problems

As the Noom diet can reduce or bring down inflammation of muscles, bones, and tissues, it can also stop or reduce the intensity of other problems such as arthritis, muscle pain, back pain, breathing issues, etc. Losing weight will also help reduce the stress on your joints and make you much more active, fresh, and quick.

Stomach

The core nature of the Noom diet plays a vital role in changing how you eat, digest, and use food. Instead of feeding yourself empty calories in the form of harmful foods, the diet focuses on the green category of food, which contains high amounts of fruits and vegetables. These food items can keep your gut happy, and your digestive system will be clean as a flute. It can also help with other problems such as IBS, constipation, and other stomach ailments. The green category food is rich in iron, making it good for people with iron deficiencies or other blood-related problems. The high amounts of fiber in the green category of foods will prevent constipation and regulate your digestive system.

Benefits from Red Items in the Noom Diet Plan

Unlike other diet plans, the Noom diet does not restrict you from eating any foods. This includes the foods available in the red category as well. The red category, also known as the orange category, contains food items that are high in calories and low in nutrients. But not all these products are low in nutrients. Various nuts and butter are full of nutrients and can be consumed in moderation. Another benefit of the red category is that you can consume anything you want, albeit you are always aware of how much to consume without overdoing or overstepping your diet.

Chapter 11:

Noom Diet for Weight Loss/Management

The Promise

Most diets focus on cutting out certain things from your meals. These include fats, calories, carbs, sugar, etc. this is done to help you lose weight. However, the Noom diet is different. It is a weight loss app like no other, as it uses a psychological approach to change your eating habits so that you can make changes in your lifestyle. According to the website, Noom is not just trying to change how you eat but also how you think.

The idea of keeping an eye on what, how, and why you eat is not new, but what makes Noom different is that it is convenient and user-friendly. This is why it is one of the most downloaded health apps.

The Noom weight loss plan is a comprehensive plan that incorporates exercise, food, and mental health. In this program, your behavior is to be changed so that you don't just lose weight for a short time, but experience sustained and long-term weight loss.

What You Can Eat and What You Can't

Nothing is off-limits on the Noom diet, yet it is recommended and encouraged to consume food items that are low in calories and high in nutrition. This is why the Noom diet uses a color-coded system, which was explained in detail in a previous chapter.

Level of Effort: Medium

The level of effort required for this diet is medium. You need to log in details such as food, meals, exercise, etc., regularly so that the app and the coaches can give you proper instructions and advice. Doing so won't take you more than a few minutes every day. Getting frequent advice from the coach can help you lose weight with ease.

Does It Allow for Dietary Restrictions or Preferences?

Yes, the app and the diet have various food options to follow your food philosophy without caring about what you eat. You will find something even if you eat gluten-free, vegetarian, or vegan.

What Else You Should Know

Cost. Noom is not free. After a couple of weeks, you will have to pay a subscription fee according to your plan and requirements.

Support

The app provides continuous support, encouragement, and guidance. The coaches available on the app are trained in changing behavior and working on your psychology.

Chapter 12:

Pros and Cons of the Noom Diet

This chapter contains detailed pros and cons of the Noom diet, which can help you choose whether to adopt it.

Pros

Certified Health Coaches

The biggest pro of this diet is that it is based on psychology. The Noom diet is based on cognitive behavioral therapy. The coaches are trained through a 4-week intense training program, and the app helps you learn various aspects of healthy eating. It focuses on breaking unhealthy habits with the help of certified health coaches.

Psychological Approach

Understanding your relationship with food and how eating disorders and problems occur is necessary. This is based on your behavior, ideas, and feelings associated with food and eating. With the help of psychology, you can be aware of the habits and break them if they are unhealthy. You can gain self-awareness and change the behavior that can negatively impact your health.

Long-Term Results

This diet is focused on gaining long-term results. Instead of focusing on short-term and quick weight reduction, the diet focuses on changing your habits and thinking related to food and health; thus, the results and habits can last for a lifetime.

Whole Foods

Thanks to the color strategy of Noom, the diet allows people to choose nutritious, healthy, and whole foods without compromising on taste. It satisfies your taste buds, satiates your hunger, and provides ample nutrients. It provides a record of calories so you know how many calories you can still consume without overshooting your budget. It also provides recommendations and information on preparing healthy, nourishing, and tasty meals. A community of personal trainers, health coaches, nutritionists, and other users provides constant and comprehensive encouragement and support, which can keep you motivated. It can also hold you responsible, enabling you to stay focused and dedicated.

Cons

The Noom diet has a few cons that may be a problem for some people. However, these cons are much weaker than the pros.

Price

No good thing in the world is free. Similarly, the Noom diet also comes with a monthly subscription fee of $50. It might prove to be quite costly for a lot of people. For diabetes prevention, the subscription fee may go up to $89 per month.

Virtual

If you like face-to-face coaching and prefer things on a more personalized level, then this diet may not be good for you. This app is completely virtual; even coaching from your trainer or coach is done via a chat window.

Due to COVID-19, more people have become comfortable and used to online weight loss methods and various other things. This problem may not be as severe as it used to be before.

Color-Labeling

Color labeling may benefit many but may be problematic as it may induce disordered eating patterns. This method is especially bad for people who have always had a problematic relationship with food and are prone to developing bad habits related to food.

A lot of people struggle with various problems associated with food and eating. Suppose you feel that the Noom diet and its color-labeling method may trigger you or your eating disorders. In that case, it is recommended to consult a doctor or a dietician before choosing this diet.

Meticulousness

You need to be meticulous in regularly logging your exercise, water intake, food habits, and other aspects for the app to work properly. This might be a hassle if you are lazy or forgetful.

Losing weight can take a lot of work. It needs a lot of motivation, dedication, and practice to lose weight. You need to lose weight sustainably. Otherwise, you may end up hurting yourself, or the diet or routine may not produce proper results. While it is true that you need to be meticulous about updating your stats on the Noom app regularly, this is a good habit, as it will keep you accountable to yourself. It will also help you form a lifelong routine you can follow.

Chapter 13:

Summary

The Noom diet and program can change how you look at your health and can revolutionize losing and maintaining weight. A program that is proven to work, the Noom program is based on psychology. It follows the principles of Cognitive Behavioral Therapy or CBT, making it one of the best diets you can take up.

Noom Diet

Is it Good for You?

No diet is good or bad. It depends on how you use it and your personal, physical, and emotional conditions. The Noom diet has worked for many worldwide; however, it may not work for you. It is recommended to understand the basics of the diet carefully by reading this book and then making an informed choice.

The pros and cons chapter of this book can help you understand whether the diet is suitable for you. It is possible that the diet may seem to be good for you; however, once you adopt it, you may realize that things are not working. For such people, the app offers a couple of weeks' trial to help you check whether the app and the program are good for you.

No diet is best or overall amazing. Each diet has pros and cons, which a person needs to understand properly before incorporating it into their lifestyle. This will allow you to be aware and follow the diet so that you don't end up harming or hurting yourself. This will also ensure that you get the most benefits from the diet and the exercise plan, if any.

Seeking Help

It is recommended to avoid starting any diet or making any major lifestyle changes without consulting your doctors. You must talk to a doctor, a nutritionist, and other practitioners to understand your mental, psychological, and physical condition before starting the Noom diet. There have been cases of people following random diets without consulting healthcare professionals and the diet or the healthcare regime backfiring spectacularly. It is thus necessary to talk to a doctor and run the necessary health checkups and tests before you can start the Noom program.

Conclusion

The Noom program has revolutionized the healthcare industry. It is one of the most popular diet programs available in the market. It is good because it works. As it is based on psychology, instead of focusing on quick and short-lived weight loss, the diet focuses on long-term goals so that the weight loss process is sustainable and can stay for a lifetime.

The Noom app combines a calorie counter, a weight-reduction plan, and a health counselor.

This book is ideal for people looking to adopt the Noom diet because it is well-researched and exhaustive. The book can guide you through the world of Noom and help you learn the intricacies of the same. The recipes given in this book will make the journey easy for you.

Losing weight may sound difficult, but it is not an impossible task. With dedication, practice, and a little help from the Noom app, you will surely achieve your target weight in no time.

References

Chin, S. O., Keum, C., Woo, J., Park, J., Choi, H. J., Woo, J. T., & Rhee, S. Y. (2016). Successful weight reduction and maintenance by using a smartphone application in those with overweight and obesity. Scientific reports, 6, 34563. https://doi.org/10.1038/srep34563

Pahwa, R., Goyal, A., & Jialal, I. (2022). Chronic Inflammation. PubMed; StatPearls Publishing. https://www.ncbi.nlm.nih.gov/books/NBK493173/#:~:text=Introducti on

Michaelides, A., Raby, C., Wood, M., Farr, K., & Toro-Ramos, T. (2016). Weight loss efficacy of a novel mobile Diabetes Prevention Program delivery platform with human coaching. BMJ Open Diabetes Research & Care, 4(1), e000264. https://doi.org/10.1136/bmjdrc-2016-000264

Toro-Ramos, T., Lee, D. -H., Kim, Y., Michaelides, A., Oh, T. J., Kim, K. M., Jang, H. C., & Lim, S. (2017). Effectiveness of a Smartphone Application for the Management of Metabolic Syndrome Components Focusing on Weight Loss: A Preliminary Study. Metabolic Syndrome and Related Disorders, 15(9), 465–473. https://doi.org/10.1089/met.2017.0062

Toro-Ramos, T., Lee, D.-H., Kim, Y., Michaelides, A., Oh, T. J., Kim, K. M., Jang, H. C., & Lim, S. (2017). Effectiveness of a Smartphone Application for the Management of Metabolic Syndrome Components Focusing on Weight Loss: A Preliminary Study. Metabolic Syndrome

and Related Disorders, 15(9), 465–473.
https://doi.org/10.1089/met.2017.0062

BONUS: THANK YOU

As a thank you for purchasing my book… I, Samantha Clark, offer you a FREE BONUS!!

Discover: **Fast & Flavorful Recipes for Busy Cooks**: Quick and Easy Meal Solutions for Your Busy Lifestyle

What are you waiting for? Scan the QR code now!

Or… Visit samanthaclarkbooks.com

Printed in Great Britain
by Amazon

26748155R00116